THE BUILDING BLOCKS OF

SUCCESSFUL

SELLING

By Robert K. Solomon

Mastering the Four Spheres of Success

In Sales and in Life

Cover Design by Reggie Taylor

Published and distributed by:
High-Pitched Hum Publishing
321 15th Street North
Jacksonville Beach, Florida 32250

Contact High-Pitched Hum Publishing at www.highpitchedhum.net

High-Pitched Hum
Publishing

This book is dedicated to my two wonderful daughters, Stephanie and Julie,
and to Jack Taylor, mentor, coach and friend.

ACKNOWLEDGEMENTS

This book was definitely a team effort. It would not have come to fruition without the tremendous efforts of Donna Rhodes, Connie Donaldson, Reggie Taylor, Billy Reynolds, Gray Solomon, and Joan Fischer. I am forever grateful for their efforts.

PRAISE FOR *THE BUILDING BLOCKS OF SUCCESSFUL SELLING*

"Bob's life is about building champions. Regardless of the platform –
on a football field or in relationships with customers – Bob's #1 priority
has been to develop meaningful win/win situations based on *character
first*.

THE BUILDING BLOCKS OF SUCCESSFUL SELLING extends his
personal selling experience into an easy-to-follow, common sense
approach to selling and maintaining long-term relationships. Just read
the words, incorporate them into your life, and enjoy the results."

W. Mark Broughton, President
ProCheckPlus, Inc.

"Integrity! Hard work! Strong relationships! Faith! These are just a few
of the timeless values upon which Bob Solomon has built his personal
and professional life. Having been fortunate enough to see firsthand
how successful this approach is, I can assure any reader of the pearls
this little book contains. An easy-to-read treasure, but also one that
anyone serious about living a successful life will want to refer to time
and time again.

John J. McLaughlin, Founder
MTS Environmental, Inc.

"If there was a pro-circuit for sales people, Bob would be ranked #1 in
the world! I have never seen someone having so much fun being a
salesman. As a result, he is successful, well respected and most of all,
balanced!"

William Montoya, Owner
Montoya Brower and Associates

"I have known Bob for over twenty-five years and I believe that he has lived every word...a great primer for the new sales person and a valuable course for those of us looking to revisit the basics. Looking forward to the sequel!"
Bob Williams, President
Ashbrook Simon-Hartley

"I have known Bob for the past 6 years in my practice. He is one of the most physically fit people I know for his age, living his life as he teaches others to do in this book. He is also one of the most generous people I know. As a Pop Warner Football coach he has sent a number of his kids who lack health insurance for treatment, picking up the tab. Bob is a person who lives his ideals instead of just preaching them."
Dr. Anthony Iselborn, Chiropractor
Jacksonville Jaguars Sports Medicine Physician

"This book is a "must have" that will shorten any young salesman's learning curve by years and serve as a great refresher for the seasoned salesperson. Bob's down to earth, pithy wisdom is concise and to the point. Each page contains gems of hard core experience presented in a readily accessible format."
Jim Porteous, Vice President Americas
Elimco Water Technologies, LLC

"In the reality of the engineering world, Sales Engineering is a keystone. It is the link between product design and development, and product use in the marketplace. It makes the difference between success and failure in a competitive world. Given this, it is surprising that Sales Engineering is rarely found in the curricula of engineering colleges. A notable exception is the University of Florida which has a widely enrolled minor in the subject. From 1990 to 2003, as Associate Dean for Academic Programs, I was responsible for coordinating and managing that program. And during that period, I initiated a Sales Engineering Seminar with all presentations being made by practitioners in the field. Bob Solomon was one of them. And it took little time to recognize the great wealth of knowledge Bob brought to our program. In Sales Engineering, Bob is a "Giant." His technical and personal attributes serve as a model for those planning to be engaged in sales engineering practice. His book "The Building Blocks of Successful Selling," fills a great void in text material available for use in programs such as that at UF. It is a unique and exceptional work. I do not have knowledge of any other publication that could serve as a suitable textbook for academic programs in sales engineering. It is a much needed contribution to the field, provided by an author who understands both the theory and practice of engineering sales. And, it is a book that every sales engineering practitioner should have on his or her shelf. The book deserves broad advertisement and marketing."

Warren Viessman Jr., P.E.
Professor Emeritus of Environmental
Engineering Services
University of Florida

THE BUILDING BLOCKS OF

SUCCESSFUL

SELLING

By Robert K. Solomon

Mastering the Four Spheres of Success

In Sales and in Life

ABOUT THE AUTHOR

Born and raised in Jacksonville, Florida, Bob Solomon graduated with a B.A. in history from the University of Richmond, which he attended on a football scholarship. Soon after graduation he found his passion involved working with people, and that lead him to a career in sales.

Bob is one of the most dynamic sales people in the environmental industry, respected nationally for his success and leadership in the field. With more than 40 years of experience in all facets of sales training, management and consulting, the bulk of Bob's career as a sales professional has been spent at MTS Environmental, a Manufacture's Representation Firm he joined in 1979. Over the years, he earned a reputation as a person of integrity with an unwavering commitment to his customers and their satisfaction.

Bob is now the CEO and owner of MTS Environmental which is one of the leading environmental sales firms in the nation.

As a regularly featured speaker at the University of Florida, he has received accolades for his relaxed style, humor and real-world advice. His thought-provoking lectures "Everyone is a Salesman Like It or Not" and "The Psychology of Sales" broke new ground. As Bob listened and observed, he wrote and rewrote about what he believed to be the common steps to success. The result is "The Building Blocks of Successful Selling," an easy-to-read primer loaded with practical tips on how to master success in sales and life.

Currently Bob enjoys mentoring young business professionals and coaching Pop Warner Football, encouraging his 30 "surrogate sons" in the development of the same timeless values you will find in the pages of this book. Bob lives in Ponte Vedra Beach, FL and has two daughters.

FOREWORD

THE BUILDING BLOCKS OF SUCCESSFUL SELLING brings something new to the business table seldom presented in university training. Business and sales are all about transactions and trust. Schools and sales training programs teach their students to listen and probe to identify customer needs, then promote their company's advantages. Bob Solomon has a different style. Still, he is one of the most successful salesmen I have ever met. His volume and profit margins are always at the highest levels. So, how does he do it?

I think it comes from Bob's experience and dedication to team sports. First, he always looks upon his relationship with the customer as a team activity, and the customers generally reciprocate. He also acts as a coach to many of his customers – bringing them contacts and situations that allow them to improve their performance with their own customers. Bob acts as a facilitator and a mentor. He doesn't really teach or lecture his clients. Instead he opens doors for them and exposes them to new possibilities. In return they become more receptive to whatever Bob brings into their sphere; they are on the same team.

It really comes down to trust. Companies spend billions of dollars on promotional tools and sales consultants whose sole function is to build trust with potential customers. That's what all those brochures, ad campaigns, point-of-purchase displays and websites and even corporate annual reports are supposed to be doing: building trust with your target customer group.

Bob performs that function merely by the way he conducts himself with consistency and high ethical standards within his day-to-day life. He says what he does and does what he says. This kind of character is something that is becoming all too rare in our modern high-stress, high-turnover lifestyle. In government, in professional organizations, in corporations, and most social institutions, too many of us are too willing to sacrifice our personal integrity for the fast buck. Like

Aesop's *Tortoise and the Hare* we often find that slow and steady does win the race.

Dependability penetrates accounts, establishes true relationships, promotes negotiations and results in win-win decisions. And after all, there are no win-lose situations. If you are a long-term thinker you know that there are only win-win and lose-lose results.

This is a book that truly belongs on every salesman's nightstand. A five-minute read every night will help you improve your "soft" skills – and in the end these may be the only real skills that count, because they overshadow all the "hard" data you may try to present to your customer. It's a five-minute investment that will pay for itself many times over.

Michael Dillon, President
Seepex Inc.

I BELIEVE
In the sacredness of a promise, that a man's word should be as good as his bond, that character, not wealth or power or position, is of supreme worth.

John D. Rockefeller

INTRODUCTION

I wrote this book as a common sense guide for those individuals who would like to become sales professionals. It is about the fundamentals of selling, with emphasis on the philosophy and attitude necessary for building and maintaining a successful career in sales.

My experience has taught me that learning the *techniques* of selling is not enough. This book is not only about techniques; it is about the actual building blocks for a successful *career* in sales.

I believe many people in sales attempt to sell before they have learned the basics of how to deal with people. Vince Lombardi built a football dynasty for the Green Bay Packers by training professional football players in the basics of blocking and tackling. He did not try to reinvent the wheel. He won two Super Bowls and numerous NFL titles just by going back to basics.

Most salespeople receive on-the-job training for sales techniques, and there is no substitute for experience. However, I hope that this book will give you a leg up on the basic concepts of building lasting *relationships*, which are the key to successful sales careers.

I designed this book as a glossary of useful terms arranged in alphabetical order to make it a quick reference guide. The definitions within are not hard and fast rules. They are not carved in stone. They are the summary of my experience of what it takes to be successful in sales, based on my 40 years in a highly rewarding sales career.

It is my intent for each concept to stand on its own. Taken all together the book is presented as a system for effective living, and when used in that fashion it will provide you with a rich and abundant life, not only in your business, but in your community and your social and family life as well.

During the writing of the book, my ideas and concepts about the sales arena were tested. My deeper awareness of the basics encouraged me to put them into practice more consciously than ever. Before the book was finished, I received my largest order ever.

Take whatever you want and need from this book, and incorporate it into your own personal style. I can't promise you instant success, but I do promise that if you *use* this information consistently over a period of time, you will outdistance your competitors and you will enjoy a more profitable sales career. You will, more importantly, give yourself the best gift of all: the inner peace that comes with the assurance that you are striving to become all you can be, and seeking greater satisfaction in all areas of your life.

Bob Solomon

THE FOUR SPHERES OF SUCCESS

Just as a soldier goes off to boot camp for basic training to prepare himself for battle, an aspiring salesman should consider putting *himself* through basic training – both prior to and throughout his career. This training will ensure that he is completely confident in his endeavors and will help to eliminate the obstacles to success that he himself creates. Successful basic training underlies success in sales and involves understanding and mastering four essential areas: intellectual growth, physical wellbeing, emotional growth, and spiritual fitness.

INTELLECTUAL GROWTH

Intellectual growth should never end with formal education. You should develop a lifelong commitment to investing in your own continuing growth. If sales is your chosen career, if this is where you want to be and this is where your gifts lie, then a large part of your intellectual efforts will automatically go into studying your chosen field. This includes salesmanship in general, your products, your industry, your competition, your own company, the economy, and basics of human relations and psychology.

Subscribe to magazines that relate to your industry to keep abreast of changing events, products and markets. Listen to self-help recordings. Read business, news and general magazines to help you grow as an individual. When you travel, carry a recording device so you can capture ideas that come to you.

I had a professor in graduate school who said that the three keys to intellectual growth are: reading, reading, and reading. Reading engages the mind and requires you to think – much more so than passively watching a TV screen. You should read for entertainment and relaxation as well as for growth. Reading for enjoyment can be a form of meditation that will help reduce stress by taking your mind off your job and other pressure-related issues.

I am convinced that with the proper motivation and interest, you can learn any subject. If you are willing to invest the time and make the effort, you can master new knowledge and develop new skills. Too many of us grew up believing we weren't intellectually gifted. The truth is you can accomplish almost anything you set your mind to. How you use what is between your ears is vastly more important in predicting success than a score on an IQ test. Truly, the limits we have in our lives are those limits we place on ourselves. Someone said, **"Argue for your limitations, and they are yours."** Once you understand this and truly believe it, you can remove any obstacle to intellectual growth you may have placed on yourself.

Throughout high school and college I struggled with math, believing that I just wasn't mathematically oriented. I accepted this fact and proved it on every report card. It wasn't until I decided to start working on a graduate degree that I really applied myself with proper interest and motivation to break through the barrier of being "mathematically challenged". I ended up making an "A" in the course. Before, I would have grudgingly accepted a lower score, believing that I simply wasn't good in math. I probably would have had to struggle with mathematics for the rest of my life.

PHYSICAL WELL-BEING

It is unfortunate that in our culture people are judged by their appearance. First impressions are lasting impressions. We never get to make a second first impression.

Your physical condition is part of the image you portray. People who are energetic and sharp physically are often perceived as being mentally sharp as well. Many successful people are often reasonably trim as well as aerobically fit and energetic. I strongly recommend a physical fitness program. Thirty minutes of aerobic exercise three or four times a week will keep you physically fit. Always consult a physician before embarking on a fitness program.

Many people would *like* to be physically fit but never actually begin a program. The biggest excuse people give for not exercising is that they don't have time. If you break a week down, there are 168 hours available for use. Subtracting 50 hours of work and 56 hours for sleep leaves some 62 hours available for leisure, entertainment, and miscellaneous pursuits. We are looking at investing only two of those 62 hours per week toward becoming physically fit. That's a pretty small price to pay for the benefits you will receive.

Physical fitness is a lifetime commitment. I played football through high school and college and was in reasonably good shape although I weighed in excess of 220 pounds when I played college football. Once I quit playing football I no longer had the motivation to stay in condition. It's amazing how fast my chest fell to my stomach.

I went several years after graduating from college with no physical fitness program and it showed rather quickly. I didn't gain weight; it just shifted around. Today, some 40 years later, I believe I'm in better shape than I was back in high school and college when I was actually playing football. I've maintained a program for the past 32 years of walking three miles, four times a week; weight training three times a week; along with yoga and tai chi daily. Since embarking on this physical fitness program 32 years ago, I have stopped a two-pack-a-day cigarette habit and maintained my weight at 185 pounds over the past 32 years. Additionally my resting pulse rate has gone from 86 beats a minutes to 52 beats a minute.

Being physically fit has a positive carryover into being emotionally fit as well. A good strenuous physical fitness program will reduce and release the pressures and stresses of life. Being physically fit allows one to think more clearly and quickly than when in a sedentary, lethargic condition. Being fit actually gives you more energy. With the extra energy, you find you have more productive time available to you each day.

If you don't enjoy jogging, try walking at a fast pace. If you don't enjoy walking, try swimming. If you don't enjoy swimming, try biking. If you don't enjoy those forms of exercise then try racket ball, tennis, squash or handball. Any form of exercise that you can maintain at an elevated heart rate for 30 minutes will give you physical and cardiovascular fitness.

Being physically fit may not add additional years to your life, but it will certainly add life to your years!

EMOTIONAL GROWTH

The greatest drawback to successful living is the lack of positive self-worth. This quality can be the determining factor between success and failure.

If we are truly responsible for who we become, then why do some people seemingly choose lives of failure, sadness and despair, while others choose to create lives full of joy, accomplishment and self-fulfillment? The common thread interwoven through successful living is healthy self-esteem. Thus, removing the emotional obstacles that negatively affect self-worth is of primary importance.

Successful people are emotionally fit. Successful salesmen carry around very little negative emotional baggage. If it comes to your attention that any negative behavior or belief is limiting your potential or your success, seek help. The bravest, most successful people I know are those who admit that they need to make a change and then do whatever it takes to accomplish this change.

The means to increase personal growth for emotional fitness are many and varied. The self-help sections in bookstores are exploding with titles zeroing in on a number of approaches to growth. There are many different kinds of counselors, therapists, and life coaches, as well as personal growth and self-help seminars.   For the successful, life is a continual process of bringing our self-defeating behaviors into awareness, acknowledging them, letting them go, and developing more effective behaviors in their place.

From early childhood through early adulthood, I believed that I was condemned to living with a bad temper. I thought that was a part of my personal makeup that I would simply have to accept about myself. I didn't realize that the personal tragedy of losing my father in a plane crash at the age of seven had made me a very angry young man. I was angry at the world for the death of my father. It wasn't until I came to terms with that anger and understood its source that I could release myself from the "angry young man" persona and get rid of the illusion that I was just an ill-tempered human being.

Many of us carry around such self-limiting illusions.   The process of emotional growth is to get rid of those illusions and myths we've been carrying around like excess baggage, and become our true selves.

SPIRITUAL FITNESS

By spiritual fitness I do not mean you have to become a Bible-toting salesman. What I do mean is living your life and conducting your business and social life according to basic spiritual values, treating everybody, including yourself with respect.   Treating yourself and others respectfully and developing a reputation for being ethical and fair in your business and social dealings are essential to true success. It is important that your customer develop a sense of trust and confidence that you will always have their best interests in mind.

Just how does one go about developing positive values in life? Primary values are learned in your family as you grow up. Some are passed on to us from churches, schools, or social institutions. However, you can and should become responsible for finding and developing your own highest value system.

There are many books published on values; there are seminars given on values and ethics; values are preached from every church and synagogue. You can effectively learn a system of values by surrounding yourself with people of high moral fiber, who practice what they preach.

Finally, you can turn to a power greater than yourself. By placing your faith in that power, however you may conceive that power to be, you will find your life changing. Instead of confusion you will find direction; instead of anxiety, peace; instead of arrogance, humility. You will begin to replace hate with love, insecurity with confidence, judgment with compassion. In the end you will find freedom. The freedom to emerge from the myth of the person you thought you were into the person you actually were created to be is an experience not to be missed.

A

ABILITY

There is a common misconception that certain people are born to a career in sales. Let me assure you, there is no such thing as a born salesperson.

People think that to be successful in sales you must be smooth talking, extroverted, and extremely attractive. I can tell you for a fact that I have known extraordinarily successful salesmen and women who were introverted, who stuttered, and who were not as conventionally attractive as others. I myself am living proof.

Developing our gifts, rather than relying on first impressions of how we look and what we say, will determine just how far we can go. Ability is something to be developed, rather than something we are born with. Those who are willing to put in the long, hard hours, working to develop their skills and gifts to the maximum potential will be successful in any field or endeavor they choose.

I submit to you that if you will apply what you have learned from this book on a daily basis, the payoffs will be immeasurable.

In his book *The Warrior Athlete*, author Dan Millman asserts that life develops according to what is demanded of it. No demand, no development; small demand, small development. Your success depends upon the demands you are willing to place upon yourself. Within the bounds of its natural capacity, the human organism will adapt to the demands made upon it. This is the law of accommodation.

The values and concepts outlined in this book form a system of successful selling. If utilized consistently, this system will provide what you demand. Just like the professional tennis player who practices his or her serve until it becomes as natural as breathing, you will, by utilizing this system over and over throughout your career, develop your own natural selling style. After a while, this system will become so ingrained you won't have to stop and think about it. Being patient, respectful, and ethical in your business practice will simply become a natural part of who you are.

ADVERSITY

Retired Notre Dame football coach Ara Parsegian said, "Adversity elicits talent which under prosperous conditions would have remained dormant."

Anyone can hold the helm during calm seas. The true professionals rise to the task when faced with adversity. They search for solutions, rather than staying mired in the problem. The true professional takes responsibility for resolving problems rather than blaming others for the current situation.

Professionals look for the opportunities provided by adversity rather than allowing themselves to be overwhelmed by circumstances. They remain calm in the face of the storm.

I remember being in our production manager's office years ago when an irate customer called. He was upset that we had sent the wrong equipment to his job site and he was ranting and raving about his problem. The production manager told him that *he* didn't have a problem. The problem was ours, and we were going to resolve it. This approach took the customer off the offensive so a solution could be worked out. Had our production manager sunk to the customer's level and started yelling back, he would have set up an adversarial confrontation. Even if the problem had ultimately been resolved, we would have lost the customer's future business.

The only way we can set up an adversarial confrontation is if we choose to join in. Look for opportunities to resolve problems, rather than becoming a part of them.

AMBITION

Ambition is a positive motivator. Ambition is the desire to do more, be more or have more than you have right now; it is a key ingredient for success in sales. However, heed these two warnings about ambition:

1) Always be sure that your ambitions are for those things that *you* truly want. If your ambition is set on what someone else wants, you will unknowingly sabotage your own efforts.

2) Avoid becoming overly ambitious. Too much ambition can cause you to be unethical or unconcerned about others,

leading to a lifestyle that embraces flash over substance, money over virtue, greed over conscience and a philosophy of winning at any cost.

If you make a win/win philosophy an integral part of your ambition, you will earn your customer's trust – and your own self-respect.

ANGER

Anger is a luxury that the professional salesperson cannot afford. You will notice that successful people do not show anger. Most successful people seldom become angry, and they have learned how to handle it when they do.

Your job as a salesman is to create a win/win situation with your customer, and there is no place for anger in this relationship. If you have a quick temper, buy a punching bag or participate in an active sport that allows you to release your aggressions against an inanimate object.

Years ago when I was selling paper to printing companies, I had one customer who gave me only one order a year, and that was for a type of paper he was unable to buy from anyone else. The rest of his paper needs were supplied by my competitors at the cheapest price.

One night he called me at my home. My competitor had let him down and could not deliver his paper. In order to meet the grand opening of a bank he needed it first thing the next morning. At 5:30 that morning I went to the warehouse, got the paper, cut it to the size he needed it, wrapped it, put it in the trunk of my car and delivered it to him.

I thought I was his Knight in Shining Armor on the White Horse. Certainly, in the future he would be doing a lot more business with me because of my excellent service. However, the next time I went to call on him with this newfound relationship firmly planted in my mind, he was upset with me because, in his opinion, I had charged him two dollars too much. I looked on the shelves and saw his new supply of paper, once again from my competitors at the lowest price.

I came unglued. I let him know in no uncertain terms what lengths I had gone to and the inconvenience it had caused me, all to save him the embarrassment of not having the printed material ready for the bank's grand opening. I let him know I felt used and did not appreciate him being so picky as to complain that we overcharged him two bucks after all my efforts. I stormed out of the room.

Later I learned that he had found someone else to supply the one paper he had been ordering from me. I realized the hard way, early in my career, that self-righteous indignation has no place in business dealings. If I really wanted his business I needed to be aware of the fact that he was a price buyer. Unless I had the better price, he was always going to buy from my competitor, until my competitor went out of business or increased prices. I should have been satisfied to continue to service him when he had emergency needs and with that one order a year, hoping that one day my competitor would stumble and that customer would then look to me based on all the services I had provided him over the years.

Instead, anger and taking it personally cost me a customer. Giving in to anger always means learning the hard way.

APOLOGIZE

It takes a big person to admit when they are wrong, and it takes a bigger person to apologize to the person they have wronged. When you realize that you have offended another person, you should make amends as soon as possible.

Your apology needs to be sincere and heartfelt, given with the other person's feelings in mind and not just to relieve your guilt.

APPOINTMENTS

Always, always make an appointment – one that is convenient for your customer. Never, ever walk in unannounced; "just dropping in" shows that you have a disregard for your customer's time.

Arrive for your appointment fifteen minutes before scheduled. This gives you time to collect your thoughts and prepare for your call. You can review your notes from your previous sales calls with this customer, study points that need to be covered in this meeting, and review new and interesting ideas about your products. This fifteen-minute window also allows you leeway in the event you get tied up in traffic.

Allow sufficient time in between appointments. Remember, some appointments will run over your scheduled time. Allow for that possibility.

If you show up as suggested, fifteen minutes early, neither announce yourself nor have the secretary announce you. Sometimes, being fifteen minutes early and being announced is just as irritating as being fifteen minutes late, as your customer has probably scheduled their day and may need that time frame before your call to meet their own priorities.

When you arrive, simply say to the secretary "I'm here, I'm early, I don't want to be announced until the prescribed time." Use this time to collect and prepare your thoughts.

Always call if you're going to be late for an appointment. The customer may have a tight schedule, so leave the option open to reschedule if he or she wishes. If you're going to be too late, they will feel pressured. Simply say: "I'm running about twenty minutes late. If that's inconvenient I'll be glad to reschedule another appointment at your convenience." Let them make the decision.

There will be times when you completely forget an appointment.

You may have scheduled it and written it down a week in advance. You may even have it on your calendar, and then something will come up – an event, an unscheduled trip, whatever the case may be – and you absolutely forget to make that call.

When you realize what you've done, immediately call and apologize. Don't try to make excuses, and don't try to bluff your way out of it. Simply say, "I've got to be completely honest with you, I blew it. I completely forgot our scheduled appointment. I apologize; I assure you it won't happen again. I'm certainly sorry for any inconvenience that I may have caused you." It was rude to forget the appointment, but it's even ruder and insults your customer's intelligence when you try to bluff your way through the explanation of why you didn't show up.

Apologize, and move forward.

ARROGANCE

People enjoy doing business with successful people. People enjoy being around winners. However, there is a difference between a successful attitude and outright arrogance. Arrogance implies superiority and, ironically, is usually based on feelings of insecurity. Truly successful people respect *all* other human beings as well as themselves.

Ask yourself if *you* would do business with someone whose attitude says, "You're not as good or as important as I am." One of the keys to success in sales is a basic assumption of equality between yourself and others.

The arrogant are usually overbearing. This is the last image you would ever want to project to customers. Other characteristics include disdainful, superior, haughty and lordly. Would you like your customer to use those adjectives when describing you?

Remember: **Arrogance is God's gift to shallow people.**

ASSERTIVE vs. AGGRESSIVE

An assertive person is perceived as someone who is both self-confident and fair. An aggressive person, on the other hand, is perceived as someone who is pushy, self-centered and wants things to go only one way – their way.

The goal is to be assertive in those situations where it is required without stepping on the toes of others. An example: A customer is trying to get you to lower your price, and you have no room to move. You simply state that the price you have given them is the absolute best you can provide. Explain that when you originally quoted the price, you understood at that time that cost was important, and you gave them your lowest possible price up front with no room to cut it.

Alternatively, you could say "Look, that's my best price offer. Take it or leave it. In fact, if you don't buy today my price is going up, so make up your mind!"

The differences are obvious, though I have exaggerated to make the point. Always think about what you are going to say and how it will be received. Think in terms of how your customer will be left feeling after you have made your statement, and you will be admired as assertive, not resented as aggressive.

ASKING

So many first-time salesmen go out into the field and call on customers armed with product knowledge, a sense of confidence about themselves and the company represent, competitive pricing, and quality products. They provide excellent service after the sale – but they never seem to get the business. What is the mystery here?

There is an old story about a personable salesman who went about his territory for six months calling on customer after customer. Both he and his sales manager were bewildered because he never received any business. Finally, his manager called on those same customers and said, "Tell me about our salesman Charlie. Is he doing a good job?"

"Oh, yes. Yes, he does a great job."
"Does he explain our products well?"
"Oh, very well. He seems to really know his products."
"Is he pleasant?"
"Oh, he's very pleasant. We all really like Charlie. He's great. We enjoy him calling on us."
"Well, let me ask you one more thing. Why hasn't Charlie ever

gotten your business?"

The customer thought for a minute, and he said, *"He's never asked us for our business."*

This rings so true with many new salesmen. They make their calls, they make their presentation, they represent their products well, they put the customer at ease – and then they get up and leave without ever asking for the order.

Yes, they never ask the customer for his business – so they don't get it. One of the most important things in sales is to remember to ASK for the order. The easiest and simplest way to ask is to make this statement at the end of your presentation:

"Is there anything else I need to do for us to do business together?"

This question gives the customer two options. They can tell the salesman exactly what needs to be done so that the deal can be set. Or they can say "No, there's nothing else. Let's do business." Both of these are positive responses.

Most of us avoid asking for a commitment because we dread hearing the word *no*. As a new salesman, know that you will hear the word *no* a lot, and that usually it's not a personal rejection.

Remember, it is very, very rare to hear a *yes* if you have failed to ask the question.

ATTITUDE

Whoever said, "Attitude is more important than Fact" had it right. Your attitude is the one thing always under your control. We cannot always control circumstances, but we can always control how we *respond* to circumstances.

Remember the last two lines of *Invictus*, the poem many of us had to memorize back in school? "I am the Master of my Fate/ I am the Captain of my Soul." Well, I have learned that it is better for me to read these lines like this: "I am the Master of my Attitude/ I am the Captain of my Gratitude."

Gratitude for all that you have, plus a positive attitude of expectancy for the good things to come, make for an unbeatable approach to your career and your life. In the words of Norman Vincent Peale:

"When you wholeheartedly adopt a "with all your heart" attitude and go all out with the positive principle, you can do incredible things."

AUTOMOBILES

Your transportation is part of the image that you project. It is important that the vehicle you drive reflects success without being ostentatious or showy.

There is a temptation when you start making money to buy a

"fancy" car, and there is nothing wrong with driving a Jaguar, Ferrari, or a Porsche – unless your customers drive Fords. If they do, make your expensive car the family car.

For business choose a non-sporty automobile with classic lines, aiming for an impression of quality rather than flash. The look should be classy, but conservative. Choose a vehicle that provides comfort for both your customer and yourself.

Cleanliness and orderliness are also part of your image. Keep your car clean and neat. The condition of your car makes a definite statement about you as a person.

I had a very good friend who worked for Ford Lincoln Mercury and was given a brand new Lincoln Continental Mark II each year. When he was finished with it his car would be offered to middle management. If middle management did not pick it up it would be sold on the outside at a much-reduced cost. He brought the car by my house one day.

It was silver with red pinstripes. I lusted for that car. A chance existed that it would be passed over by middle management and I could buy it for approximately $16,000.00 – less, at the time, than you would pay for a new Ford of Chevrolet. As luck would have it, one of the middle managers bought the car and I bought a station wagon. As time went on, I listened to the people I called on talk about my competitors, who were driving Mercedes, Jaguars or BMWs. I could detect resentment in their comments.

You could tell they were put off by the fact that they,   the customers, were buying goods and services from salespeople who were driving big, fancy cars while they drove the smaller cars they could afford. They resented that comparison.

I learned a very important lesson by listening to my customers' feelings about my competitors' fancy show cars. I thank my lucky stars that the middle manager bought the Lincoln Continental and I didn't have to learn the lesson the hard way.

HOW DO I RATE? HOW CAN I IMPROVE?

ABILITY_____

_____

ACCOMMODATION_____

_____

ADVERSITY_____

_____

AMBITION_____

_____

ANGER_____

_____

APOLOGIZE_____

_____

APPOINTMENTS_____

_____

ARROGANCE_____

_____

ASSERTIVE VS. AGGRESSIVE_____

_____

ASKING_____

_____

ATTITUDE_____

_____

AUTOMOBILE_____

_____

B

BODY LANGUAGE

Pay attention to body language. Your customer's body will tell you when they are listening and when their attention is elsewhere. It will tell you when they are confused, when they are interested, when they are getting your point, and when they need clarification.

In other words, your customer's body will usually tell you what's going on in their mind regardless of what words are coming out their mouth. It is well worth your while to pay attention and use this information to your best advantage.

A good salesman also remembers that his or her *own* body language is broadcasting information to his customer. I recommend using a video or getting feedback from a close friend to learn which signals you send with your body, consciously or not. You want always to project positive verbal and non-verbal feelings and messages. The messages and feelings you send out will usually come back to you in the same manner as "like attracts like."

Look for the following signs and take the appropriate corrective action when you see them displayed in your customer:

1. Sitting with arms folded across the chest: it may mean they have closed their minds.

2. Drumming their fingers on the desk: it could indicate they are irritated.

3. Constantly glancing at their watch: they may be losing patience, and you may be running out of time.

4. Repeatedly looking out the window: they may be bored. You may not be holding their attention.

5. Failing to make eye contact with you: it may mean they don't believe what you are saying.

You can use these guidelines to check on how you are progressing in establishing rapport with the client. If any of these should pop up, use them as red flags to let you know that the sales call is not moving along well.

You may wish to ask some questions to bring your customer back into the conversation. Ask them what they think, ask them for their opinion. Remember that you want *them* to do the talking; you want them to let you know what their needs are. To this end you need to constantly be aware of their feelings. If you ignore their body language, you may never reach them and wind up wondering in frustration why your competitor got the sale you missed.

Remember, it is up to you as a salesman to capture and hold your customer's interest, to keep them from being bored, and to avoid encroaching on their time. Certainly you want to avoid irritating your client and keep the sales call moving along in a timely manner and a positive direction. When you see these body language warning signals, it is up to you to adjust the communication. The ball is in your court to make the necessary adjustments to bring the focus back into a positive arena.

Just as you will be attempting to read and interpret your customer's body language, remember they can also read yours. So be careful as to the messages your own body conveys.

HOW DO I RATE? HOW CAN I IMPROVE?

BODY LANGUAGE

_____

_____

_____

_____

_____

_____

C

CAN'T

Remove this word from your vocabulary. No customer or sales manager will tolerate the use of *can't* from a salesman. There is a solution to every problem, so always look for the positive outcome rather than giving up too soon.

When a customer asks for terms that you know from previous experience that the factory won't accept, don't just blurt out that you can't do it. Tell your customer you will talk with the factory. If the factory still won't go along with the customer's terms go back to them with a compromise position. If you say you can't from the very start, you may prevent future negotiations. By offering a compromise you keep the communication moving and open.

CELL PHONE

In this age of instant communication and 24/7 accessibility the cell phone can be the salesman's greatest tool – and the arena where courtesy and good manners are most easily abused.

We've all witnessed it. Maybe we've even done it. A face-to-face business meeting is taking place. Important issues are being discussed, and the customer is intently focused. Communication between salesman and client is flowing easily.

Then—the cell rings. The salesman snatches it up immediately. The live, waiting customer is put on "hold" indefinitely while he talks on and on and on. Sometimes, this happens without apology or even an "excuse me."

The present client sits forgotten while the salesperson deals with someone, or some issue, he obviously considers to be more important. Our customer may start to do a slow burn. At the very least, he will begin to disengage mentally from the transaction.

When did this behavior come to be the norm? In the "olden days" salespersons were taught that attending to the customer in front of them always took precedence over the telephone call. If a call had to be answered, it was done discreetly to let the person on the other end know that the salesman was attending to the needs of a "live" customer.

Today, the opposite is coming to be the case, not only in the business world but in our whole society. Technology should not be the master, but the servant. Use technology; don't let it use you!

CLOTHING/DRESS

The style of your dress, the clothes you choose and your personal grooming all make a definite statement about who you are.

Your dress generally is determined not only by your own personal philosophy, character and personality but is also affected by the tradition of your company and the customs of the businesses upon which you call.

If your company and customer base are both conservative (e.g. banking and insurance industries), your business dress should also be conservative in style. If you are employed in one of the entertainment or design fields, your clothing might be less conservative. I personally work in a conservative-oriented field. Designer clothes are not appropriate in this type of business, since it involves calling on engineers in a technical field. For years I have owned a tan suit, a blue suit, a blue blazer and a pair of gray slacks. As a rule, I can make numerous combinations, all of which are conservative, in style, and in good taste.

I suggest investing from the beginning in the best quality you can afford. My second suggestion is to take care of your investment. Notice the condition of your clothes. Are they neatly pressed? Anything frayed? Any buttons missing?

The rule for personal appearance is: people like to do business with winners, so dress like one and you will be ahead of the game.

In the late Sixties double-breasted suits were a popular fad. I've always been naturally conservative and my clothing reflected that taste. A good friend talked me into buying a couple of double-breasted pinstriped suits. I bought them, wore them for a while, but never felt comfortable in them. I didn't project the image that was the real me. I felt that I looked like a con artist, and I'm sure this was projected in my mannerisms and the way I carried myself when I wore those suits. When selecting clothing, choose items that make you feel comfortable and confident.

COLD CALLS

Probably one of the most difficult, and sometimes terrifying, things for a new salesman to do is to make a cold call. What follows is a technique that I use which takes pressure off both myself and the customer.

Calling on a new prospect, I introduce myself on the telephone and request a meeting for introductory purposes. My conversation is basically simple. "Good morning. My name is Bob Solomon. I work for XYZ Manufacturing Company. I'm new in the territory and would like to stop by and introduce myself to you. I'll be in town next Tuesday and Wednesday. Is either one of those days more convenient for you?"

This approach puts the customer at ease. You are not trying to sell them something on the first call; you just want to come by and meet him.

Very few people can refuse this offer of an introduction. Through constructive listening during this introductory call, you will discover what your potential customer's needs are, what products and services they are currently using, and how you could possibly become a part of their business in the future. On your next call, you can begin presenting your own products and services. The first call, the cold call, should only be exploratory. The unstated purpose of the meeting is to find out just what it would take to get this customer's business. The call itself should be purely social.

COMMISSIONS

It is important that you have a clear commission or incentive policy established with your company. The commission should be set objectively and fairly, and it should be one that gives you the opportunity to maximize your earnings based on your productivity.

As a commissioned salesman, you should set definite goals as to how much money you want to earn. You will be amazed how your work and effort will expand to meet those goals. If you have no earning goals, you may not work as productively as you could. By establishing those clear-cut goals you will set your efforts in that direction, and more times than not you will accomplish them if you follow the guidelines presented in this book.

COMMITMENT

Customers want to do business with people who are willing to make, and keep, commitments. Customers ultimately want to know that you have a firm commitment to them.

Customers take notice of the commitments you make to yourself, your company, your family, your friends, and your community. Customers intuitively know that if you are unwilling to make commitments in other areas of your life you probably won't make a commitment to them and their needs.

Look at professional athletes. The ones who demonstrate commitment sustain their careers. How many athletes can you name who emerge from college having all the ability in the world, but never make it professionally? Usually you can trace this failure back to their lack of personal commitment to success.

I suggest you regard commitment as a quality that creates possibilities rather than something that limits you. If your commitment is clear, a means of achieving this commitment will appear. Your customer wants to know that when the going gets tough, they can count on you to get the job done regardless of any difficulties.

COMMUNICATION

The success or failure of any communication, written or verbal, is determined by the *response* it elicits. It is up to you to be sure that your communications are clear, comprehensible and positive. Analyze the message you are about to give *before* you speak or write. Make your communication honest and straightforward, with no room left for misunderstanding.

Watch for any body language and/or verbal implications that your message is not being received. When you do get these signs, say "I'm not making myself clear. Let me rephrase that." Continue rephrasing your message until you're assured that your customer gets it.

COMPETITORS/COMPETITION

For many people, the challenge of competition is one of the major appeals of a career in sales. Sales-minded individuals like the idea of being on the firing line – the challenge of winning and losing. They like the idea of putting forth their maximum effort against a tough competitor. Winning against strong competition can be extremely satisfying.

Competition is more than a means to provide motivation. It is important to have the respect of your competitors. It is important that your reputation be such that your competition in the marketplace says good things about you. What your competitors think of you does have an influence on buyers. It can be a cause for concern in the buyer's mind if you are not held in esteem by your competitors.

By the same token, it is important for you to refrain from maligning, criticizing or belittling your competition. Being positive about your competitors will gain you more respect than any negative aspect that you could possibly point out.

It is also crucial for you to *know* your competition – their products and how they fit or don't fit your customers' needs. This helps you understand what disadvantages there might be in the competition's product and what advantages your own product offers. Only in truly knowing your competition can you show where your product has advantages and fits your customers' needs better than do your competitors' products, and you will be able to convey this knowledge directly to your customer.

COMPETITOR PROFILE

It is as important to know your competitor as it is to know the company you work for. The following checklist will give you some direct insight into how to outmaneuver your competition.

1. Competitor's Company

Name _____

Phone: _____**Cell**_____

Address:_____

City, State, Zip:_____

2. Competitor's Products

A. _____

B_____

C. _____

D. _____

3. Competitor's Advantages

A. _____

B. _____

C. _____

D. _____

4. Competitor's Disadvantages

A. _____

B. _____

C. _____

D. _____

5. Competitor's Pricing Strategy

_____

_____

_____

6. Competitor's Financial Strength

_____

_____

(Buy one share of stock and you will receive their Annual Reports as well as their Newsletter. If stock is not available, you can get a Dunn & Bradstreet Report.)

7. Competitor's Reputation as it relates to:

    A. Service_____

    B. Quality_____

    C. Reliability_____

    D. Ethics_____

    E. Commitment_____

COMPLIMENTS

Everyone appreciates a sincere and genuine compliment. When you are sitting across the desk from your customer, you may notice pictures of their family, a tennis trophy, a company award or any other memento of which they are obviously proud. (Otherwise, they wouldn't be there.) Asking about any of these is a positive way to establish instant rapport, *if* your comments or questions reflect a sincere interest. If your comments and questions are interpreted as a sales technique, they will have a negative effect. Always letting your customer know that you are genuinely interested in them as a human being will have positive results.

CONFERENCE CALLS

When a customer has a question about your product or service, it means that they are possibly interested and are investigating your product with the potential of purchasing. A conference call is a good method of showing your customer that you understand and appreciate their sense of immediacy and that you are willing to do whatever it takes to get the best, and the most accurate, answer for them. While your customer is on the line you can reach the appropriate person at the factory and get their question answered immediately.

Not only does the conference call provide immediate resolutions to questions and issues, it also tells your client that they are of value to you. Your customer will appreciate your efforts. Guess who they will call the next time they are looking for solutions.

CONFIDENCE

As noted earlier, people enjoy doing business with winners. People enjoy doing business with successful people.

When you first go into the marketplace, you have no basis for confidence and success in the sales field. If you have never sold anything, you have no past successes from which to develop your baseline of confidence in your abilities. Therefore, in the beginning, your confidence must come from your own positive self-image.

Know that it will take time to develop a track record in sales. Allow time for this. Rejoice in the small orders as the first steps toward success. Recognize that customers generally do not develop confidence in the new salesman rapidly, but they will give you test orders. It's important that you use these test orders wisely. Take the small orders seriously, get them processed and delivered on time, and provide the quality of service that will more than satisfy the customer. Your confidence and the customer's confidence in you will grow slowly and solidly.

Do not become overconfident once your territory and your skills have broadened and you have become successful in sales. (See *Arrogance.*) Beware of assuming that a customer will continue to do business with you just because "he always has."

Complacency often results in loss of business. Continue to show your customer that they are important to you.

CONTROL

It's very important to recognize those things over which you have control, specifically your own actions and attitude, as well as things you don't. You don't have control over your competitor's pricing. You don't have control over your competitor's efforts. You need to let go of those things that you don't control and can't change, and focus on the things that you do control in order to move towards satisfactory solutions.

If you are constantly worrying about things you can't control, you will frustrate yourself, and frustration does nothing good for your effectiveness. Furthermore you are wasting energy that could be devoted toward things that you can control. So make a conscious, rational effort to determine which things come under your control and which things do not – and act accordingly.

COURTESY

Successful people respect *everybody*, in all walks of life, from the janitor to the president of the company. Truly successful people treat everyone with mutual respect and kind regard. Truly successful people realize that when others do not return their courtesy and kindness, it is not to be taken personally. Often, others are rude when they are having some kind of personal difficulty. This difficulty usually has nothing to do with you. If in doubt, ask.

One day I was delivering a proposal to a potential customer. It was to be reviewed by his engineer before it was taken to him. The engineer pointed out some mistakes in my proposal. Since time was of the essence I didn't have the opportunity to take the proposal back to corporate headquarters and have it retyped. One of the secretaries at the engineering firm overheard the conversation and said she would be glad to retype the contract.

She did so, and we gave the retyped contracts to the engineer who took the contracts in to the customer, who promptly signed them. I walked out with a very handsome order.

On my way back to the home office I thought about the kindness of that secretary. I called a florist when I got back to the office and sent a bouquet of flowers to her to let her know how much I appreciated her effort. This story got back to my customer's wife and upon meeting her one night with her husband, she remembered the story and related it. The simple act of kindness on my part brought me into a favorable light not only with the customer's wife, but with the customer as well.

CREATIVITY

Often you will find that you must create a market or create a demand for your product. You can do this by showing your customer different ways to use products which they already purchase, or you can show them different ways to use new or additional products that you are promoting. It is your responsibility to learn how your products can help the customer achieve more success in the operation of his plant, factory or office.

CUSTOMER

The customer is the key ingredient to every sale. Nothing happens in the sales business without a customer to purchase goods. One of the salesman's primary roles is to be sure that the customer is always treated fairly. They must be satisfied with your company's products, services, and pricing, and feel good about the professional relationship they have developed with you.

Keep in mind that the relationship with the customer is based on *mutual* respect. If you have a customer who consistently makes unfair demands, you must handle these situations very diplomatically. Remember that any person who repeatedly succeeds in taking advantage of you will eventually lose respect for you. Ultimately, they may even move on to your competitor.

Always try to put yourself in the shoes of your customer. Mentally move across the desk, sit in their chair and try to think as they think.

◆ What are their needs?

◆ What are their wants?

- Why should they want to do business with you?

- What might make your product more attractive to them?

- What makes your services more useful to them?

- Is the customer only looking at cost, or are they looking for quality?

- Is a shorter delivery time important?

- Are they looking for the prestige that your product may offer?

- Is energy efficiency important to them?

- Are they looking for products that are maintenance free?

- Are they looking for trouble-free products that have cost a minimum amount of down time?

The wants and needs of each customer are different. It is a very big mistake to assume that each customer wants only certain features in a product. You must get to know your customer, understand their unique needs, and deliver what they want. If you do not understand their needs and wants, I can assure you that your competitor will.

The simplest way to find out what your customer needs is to ask the question directly. "Mr. Jones, what exactly are you looking for in this product?" Then, you must listen to their answer carefully.

Many new salesmen make a mistake in not dealing with customers who are committed to the competition. In this situation, continue calling on the customer – even if it is only occasionally. If and when a customer does decide to try a new product or a different supplier, your relationship will already be established. It is a big mistake to give up on a customer simply because they appear loyal to the competition. Over time, several things can happen. Your competitor could be promoted, transferred, fired, or might simply drop out of your industry. Who will your customer turn to at that time? It has been my experience that they will turn to the salesman who has faithfully continued to call on them without any business.

Your perseverance will be rewarded. I had called upon a potential customer literally for years without getting one order. The majority of the business went to my major competitor. Because I was persistent, when my competitor fell into disfavor that customer became mine. This customer now shows me the same loyalty and allegiance that had been given to my competitor over the years, because I am now giving them the service and products that they need.

The lesson here is, persevere. Often the toughest accounts to obtain will become the toughest customers to lose, as long as you hold up your end of the bargain.

CUSTOMER PROFILE

You should come to know your customer as well as you would want to know anyone you are trying to build a long-term relationship with. The following checklist should provide you with a profile of the person with whom you are seeking to develop a long-lasting business relationship.

1. Customer

Name: _____

Title: _____

Address: _____

City, State, Zip: _____

2. Customer's Firm

Name: _____

Type of Business: _____

Address: _____

City, State, Zip: _____

Phone: _____ **Fax:** _____

Website: _____

Email: _____

3. Customer's Educational Background:

High School: _____

College: _____

Degrees: _____

4. Customer's Hobbies:

    1. _____

    2. _____

    3. _____

5. Customer's Important Dates:

Birthday: _____

Wedding Anniversary: _____

6. Customer's Entertainment Preferences:

    1. _____

    2. _____

7. Customer's Buying Habits:

    Rank in order their preference to (A) Quality, (B) Price, (C) Service, (D) Reliability, (E) Other:

    1. _____

    2. _____

    3. _____

    4. _____

8. Customer's Spouse:

Name: _____

Profession: _____

Education: _____

Hobbies: _____

9. **Customer's Children:**

Names & Ages: _____

_____

Hobbies: _____

Education: _____

This information will go a long way in giving you

insight into the person you are dealing with.

HOW DO I RATE? HOW CAN I IMPROVE?

CAN'T _____

_____

CLOTHING/DRESS _____

_____

COLD CALLS _____

_____

COMMISSIONS _____

_____

COMMITMENT_____

_____

COMMUNICATION_____

_____

COMPETITORS/COMPETITION_____

_____

COMPLIMENTS_____

_____

CONFERENCE CALLS_____

_____

CONFIDENCE_____

_____

CONTROL_____

_____

COURTESY_____

_____

CREATIVITY_____

_____

CUSTOMER_____

_____

D

DECISION MAKERS

For the newcomer, one of the trickiest aspects of sales is to discover who actually makes the buying decisions. Keep in mind that many people other than the official buyer can influence the decision to buy.

For example, if you are a copier machine salesman, you need to know that potentially everyone who uses the copy machine can take part in the ultimate decision to purchase. Therefore, it is to your advantage to get into the habit of thinking of everyone in the office as a potential component in the decision-making process. As a salesman, I suggest that you interview every potential decision-maker in each office – anyone who has the potential of using your product and, therefore, the potential to influence the final decision.

One way of doing this is to ask the person you assume to be the primary decision-maker who else would be using the machine. Tell them that you would like the other employees' input, and that you would like to discover their needs. As you move onto the next person, ask the same question. Be sure that you interview every person who will be using your product or who will influence the decision (such as the accounting department, which may have something to say about the cost of the equipment).

In a lecture I have given to sales and marketing majors in college, I ask the students to help me make a list of everyone in a typical manufacturing plant office. The list includes administrative assistants, office managers, salesmen, purchasing agents, accounts, production managers, expediters, the CEO, etc. I asked who they would focus their attention upon if they were selling a copier. Some said the purchasing agent as they controlled purchasing, some said the secretaries since they would be working directly with the machine, others said the boss since he was responsible for the final decision. It becomes obvious that everyone in the office could have *some* influence over the decision.

Even if this method seems overwhelming, the payoff is tremendous. The staff members who actually use the machine on a daily basis will appreciate your concern with their input, and most customers will be much impressed with your concern and your willingness to take the extra time to see that their needs are met.

The key is this process:

1. Identify the key decision makers.

2. Discover their needs.

3. Discover their concerns and issues.

4. Demonstrate how the features and benefits of your product will meet or exceed their demands.

5. Show how you can alleviate concerns they may have with your product or services.

Remember, decision makers are always shifting position. Just as you have developed a relationship with a key decision maker they can be promoted, transferred, fired, or lose power. Establishing relationships with a variety of decision makers within the same company helps to ensure that your business continues regardless of one individual's circumstances.

DELIVERY

Your job as a salesman does not stop after the customer has agreed to the sale. Your job continues through delivery – and beyond. Regardless of your factory's demands, changing schedules, and so forth, your customer looks directly to you to be reliable in delivering the product on time and according to specification. Passing the buck does not work here.

Remember, customers need your product in order to conduct their own business. If you don't deliver . . . if you don't deliver on time...if you don't deliver a usable product of acceptable quality...why would they continue to buy from you?

DISCIPLINE

For new salesmen, the factor that often makes or breaks their career is *discipline*.

◆ Discipline is required to be consistent.

◆ Discipline is required to be on time for your appointments.

◆ Discipline is required to make those cold calls.

◆ Discipline is required to keep all your appointments and make your rounds.

◆ Discipline is required to return phone calls in a timely manner, especially those calls from dissatisfied customers.

◆ Discipline is required to make follow-up calls after the sale to insure customer satisfaction.

◆ Discipline is required to stay on top of the factory to make sure that the order is delivered on time.

◆ Discipline is required to maintain your integrity.

◆ Discipline is required to get in those three workouts a week to keep yourself physically fit.

◆ Discipline is required to go that extra mile that your customer deserves.

Anything less that the 110% effort will cost you business and/or a relationship with your customer. This requires discipline. It takes discipline to outdistance your competitors and it takes discipline to avoid complacency later in your career. It takes discipline to be fair. And, finally, it takes discipline to maximize your potential – to be all that you are capable of being. Self-discipline is one of the highest forms of self-caring.

HOW DO I RATE? HOW CAN I IMPROVE?

DECISION MAKERS:_____

_____

DELIVERY:_____

_____

DISCIPLINE:_____

_____

E

ENTERTAINMENT

Entertaining is one of the positive, even occasionally glamorous, aspects of sales as a profession. Occasional golf, tennis, dinner, lunch or cocktails with select clients does strengthen the sales relationship. However, it is necessary to keep entertainment in balance.

The biggest caution with entertainment is to beware of ignoring the business aspects of your relationship. If your customer-salesman relationship is built primarily around entertainment, rather than quality products with competitive pricing and service after the sale, the sales relationship may be put in jeopardy.

ENTHUSIASM

Enthusiasm is another essential ingredient for the professional salesman. Genuine enthusiasm has a subtle, but positive impact on others. Enthusiasm says that you, your product and your company are winners. Remember, people enjoy doing business with winners. If you find that you yourself are not enthusiastic about your business, you need to examine why that is so.

Is the problem within you? Is the problem with the company that you represent? Is the problem that you are in the wrong industry – or the wrong profession?

Do whatever is necessary to correct the cause for your lack of enthusiasm, since this lack raises doubts in your customer's mind. If you are not positive about yourself, your business and your products, how can you expect potential customers to be enthusiastic?

ETHICS

According to Norman Vincent Peal, there are three key areas that define an ethical decision:

1. Is it *legal*?

2. Is it *fair* to all parties involved, including yourself?

3. How do you *feel* after you have made the decision? How would you feel if your decision was published in the newspaper for your family, friends and business associates to read?

If the response to all three of these questions is positive, chances are good that you have indeed made an ethical decision. If the response in any of these areas is negative, either by omission or commission, it is likely that your decision has been unethical.

Remember, your reputation will precede you in the marketplace. It does not take long in any industry for word to get around that a particular salesman is unethical.

EULOGY

Write your own eulogy, as if a friend was describing the life you lived at your funeral. Have him tell of your great success in family life, in your business, in giving back to your community, of your good health, your character, etc. Put this eulogy on your mirror and read it every time it catches your eye.

Remember, Einstein said imagination is more powerful than knowledge. Imagine the life you want, and your subconscious will direct you there.

EVALUATED/REAL COSTS

If you have chosen to be a professional salesman, I suggest that you work for a company that offers a product of high quality. Selling the best product available provides the new salesman with confidence that he otherwise might not have.

However, the best product frequently has a higher capital cost. You must, therefore, learn to sell according to Real Cost. Sell in terms of quality, competitive pricing, service, longevity of your product, reduction of cost in servicing, energy consumption, availability of service and parts, timeliness in service – in other words, be sure to include all advantages of your product.

Very often, in the long run, the best product – even if it is more expensive initially – turns out to be the least costly. It is up to you as a salesman to be sure that your customer understands and appreciates the total value of your product or service.

EXPECTATIONS

A positive expectation and a positive attitude are probably the most beneficial characteristics that a salesman can have. *Expect* to get the appointment with your customer. *Expect* that you will convince them that your product is the right product for their needs. *Expect* to be successful in obtaining the order. *Expect success*, in short, in everything you do.

Prior to any telephone or sales call, I sit quietly and visualize the entire call – every aspect of it – and I visualize a positive outcome. The power of positive expectations, a positive attitude, and positive visualization have long been recognized and utilized in athletics. Jack Nicklaus exemplified this principle. More and more businesspeople are using these powerful techniques to improve their performance, as well.

The power of self-expectation doesn't mean you can sit back in a chair and visualize and expect positive things to automatically happen in your life. You must couple *expectations* with *action*.

I try to channel all my energies – physical, mental, spiritual, and intellectual – towards effectively accomplishing my goals. Positive expectations provide the motivation, and channeling my energies provides the action to accomplish my goals. Once the task is established, I become inner directed.

Those people who don't have positive expectations usually fall short of their goals. They lose interest because they don't really believe these goals can be accomplished. In sales, this kind of negativity can be deadly.

HOW DO I RATE? HOW CAN I IMPROVE?

ENTERTAINMENT_____

_____

ENTHUSIASM_____

_____

ETHICS_____

_____

EVALUATED/REAL COSTS_____

_____

EXPECTATIONS_____

_____

F

FACIAL HAIR

Facial hair – beards and mustaches – might well be regarded negatively in the business world. Many business people feel that facial hair is used as a disguise and/or used to appear older or wiser. The best approach is a clean-shaven face if sales is your chosen profession. If you must have a beard, keep it well trimmed and neat.

Remember, while only a handful of people may be offended by facial hair, do not take the chance of losing the sale even if these are only a small percentage among those you call upon. You should never do anything that could limit your success.

FACTORY

Your relationship with your own factory is just as important as the relationship with your customer. You need a positive working relationship with the factory in order to deliver the product as promised.

Part of your job as a salesman is to let the people at the factory know how important they are, specifically how important they are to the total success of the organization. Practice rapport and your sales skills on your own support staff. Solicit their cooperation in a team effort to achieve success.

FAITH

You must have faith that if you apply the principles as outlined in this book you will achieve success. Your faith will sustain you through the difficult times when the sales are down. Your faith will sustain you as you continue to apply the principles you've learned and continue to take the success-oriented actions we have described. Without faith, you will find yourself taking shortcuts and move away from the value system that is so necessary in order to build those long-lasting, positive relationships. Without faith you will fall short of your goal of being a successful salesman.

Take heart in the fact that there are many, many other people who have used the system outlined in this book and have become tremendously successful.   Allow your faith to sustain you throughout your entire career.

FRIENDSHIP

Your job as a sales professional is not to be just a friend of the customer. However, it is often the salesperson that has taken the time to develop such a relationship with the customer who will end up getting the business.

There are several reasons for this. First, people enjoy doing business with people they like. Second, some business decisions are made based on feelings and justified later rationally or logically. Third, some products are basically equal, and the buying decision is based primarily on who has the best relationship with the customer.

Be careful that your business relationship is not founded solely on the friendship you have developed with the buyer. Your business should be based on the values that you offer. If your relationship with the buyer is strictly one of friendship, a transfer, promotion or move to another company by the buyer will surely cause you to lose the business. When the new person arrives and starts looking at the buying practices of their predecessor and realizes that the only thing you had to offer the company was a personal relationship, it will be difficult for them to justify a continued business relationship.

HOW DO I RATE? HOW CAN I IMPROVE?

FACIAL HAIR_____

FACTORY_____

_____

FAITH_____

_____

FRIENDSHIP_____

_____

G

GOALS

Goals, personal mission statements, and end-result thinking are all essential to the sales professional. Remember, positive expectations will bring positive results. If you don't know where you're going, you probably won't get there, and you'll always have the feeling that you never made it since you didn't know where you were trying to go in the first place.

Here are some general guides for goal setting:

◆ Be specific. Write down exactly what income you want to make this year, next year, and over the next five years. Write down how many sales call per week you wish to make. Describe in detail that house on the lake that you want. Be sure to fill in as many details as possible.

◆ How will you know when you have achieved your goal? Write it down. For example, "When I have a balance of $30,000 in my savings account." "When I see the deed to the property in Pacific Heights."

◆ Be sure that the goal is *yours*. If the goal is someone else's (your parent's, your spouse's, your friend's, your mentor's) you will usually sabotage yourself so that you do not in fact reach this goal. If the goal is one that you sincerely want for yourself, you will achieve it.

Henry David Thoreau stated,

"If one advances confidently in the direction of his dreams, and endeavors to live the life which he has imagined, he will meet with a success unexpected in common hours."

Twenty-eight years ago, I started running for physical fitness. This is amusing since in high school and college football I hated running. We would have to do a one-mile run at the beginning of every summer practice at the University of Richmond. I dreaded running that one mile.

Later, when I began to run again, I ran a half mile and then worked my way up to one mile, then up to three, then five. Eventually, I ran a nine-mile race called the Jacksonville River Run. After running for a couple of years I focused in on running a marathon. I established a goal of running that marathon and also established the goal of running it in just under four hours. I got a training program out of *Runner's World* magazine describing how to train for your first marathon.

It took a great deal of determination, motivation, discipline and emotional self-control to get up on those Florida mornings in June, July, August and September to train in ninety-degree temperatures. I entered and ran the New York Marathon, completing the twenty-six miles in three hours, fifty-nine minutes and twenty-four seconds – just under four hours, on the nose. I had met my goal; I ran the same pace throughout the entire marathon.

This undertaking proved to me that anything is within your reach if you establish realistic goals and allot yourself a period of time to accomplish these goals. I set a realistic goal, one that I personally wanted to accomplish. I did not run the marathon for anyone else but myself, and it gave me a sense of great personal accomplishment.

You can set goals in all areas of your life – family, business, community, personal activities – and accomplish them if you have the proper interest, motivation, discipline, realism and confidence. Goal setting should be something that you continually practice, spreading it throughout all phases of your life so that you move and grow in every area. Nothing will better ensure that you become the best person you are capable of becoming.

GREED

Remember that old adage, "What goes around, comes around?"

Your job as a professional is to protect the interest of the customer as well as your own company. If you focus on taking care of these interests, your own needs will be met as well. You will automatically win – and usually win big.

We can look back on decades, notably the 1980's, when greed seemed to displace values on the American landscape. Nothing was sacred, not the government, the ministry, or corporate America as witnessed by the crumbling empires of the savings and loan scandals involving both politicians and Wall Street.

We must all help make the 21st Century a time of return to values and of ethics taking precedence over greed. Those salesmen and women who conduct themselves accordingly will reap the rewards.

GUM CHEWING

Never, never, never walk into a customer's office chewing gum, unless you are a Georgia football fan and the customer is too.

HOW DO I RATE? HOW CAN I IMPROVE?

GOALS_____

_____

GREED_____

_____

GUM CHEWING_____

H

HABIT

People get into habit patterns and tend to buy again and again from the same source because it is convenient, easy and familiar. When a customer is buying from the competition our job as salesmen is to break that habit pattern by offering better service, better quality, and better delivery. The objective is to make their job easier because they are now doing business with you. Many times customers don't stop and think about why they are buying from the same salesmen over and over again. Never underestimate the power of habit. It is up to you to show the customer the advantages of breaking those habits by doing business with you.

You must offer more than just a warm handshake or a friendly smile in helping a customer to break away from the autopilot of old buying habits. As a professional salesman, you have to offer the total package outlined in this book. That is why you must look at the long haul rather than stay stuck with short-term vision. With persistence, discipline and patience working on your side, you will eventually break through those old habit patterns and move the customers over to your side.

HAPPINESS

"Happiness is the spiritual experience of living every minute with love, grace, and gratitude."

-Denis Waitley

Happiness is an inside job. Your big-picture goal in life should be to develop your gifts and talents to the fullest extent possible.

Many people set their goals on accumulating money, beautiful homes, fancy cars, boats, etc., thereby postponing their happiness until they have acquired these things.

A number of people I know obtained all these outward trappings of success and still had a great void inside because they had not developed themselves to their potential. "He who dies with the most toys, wins" is not a viable life philosophy if true happiness is your goal.

The only thing you truly have any control over in life is you. Successful people focus each morning on what they need to do to make themselves better people. When they maximize their potential they are contributing constructively to the lives of others as well as to their own.

Achieving your true potential and being helpful to others will ensure lasting happiness as you move through life.

HONESTY

Yes, honesty really is always the best policy, especially in business. People respect people who tell the truth.

Never bluff with answers to questions about that which you are not sure. Your potential or regular customer will appreciate your willingness to research a question that you do not know.

Consistent honesty develops a relationship based on trust. The only relationship worth having is one based on trust.

Being honest includes admitting your mistakes, acknowledging the factory's mistakes and being willing to take it on the chin to correct the situation in the best and fastest way possible.

Although being totally honest can be frightening initially, it does indeed prove to be the best policy – *and the rewards are great.*

HUMOR

A sense of humor is a valuable asset for the professional salesman. It goes a long way in establishing positive relationships with all those you are in contact with, including customers.

A good sense of humor is a good indicator of self-esteem and strong self-confidence. It is the secure person who is able to laugh at himself, and to laugh along with the group, even if they are on the receiving end of the joke.

Some people think that sarcasm is humor and try to use it that way. These individuals are perceived by the customer as being bitter and angry. Nobody likes to be around humor at the expense of others for very long. Be sure that your humor is used good-naturedly and in fun, not at the expense of another person's feelings.

HOW DO I RATE? HOW CAN I IMPROVE?

HABIT_____
_____

HAPPINESS_____
_____

HONESTY_____
_____

HUMOR_____
_____

I

IDEAS

Use ideas to make yourself valuable to the customer as a resource person. Always enter into the customer's office with something new and fresh in mind. Give them another way to use your product, another way for them to save money in their operation, or another way for them to increase their sales.

Being a resource puts you in the customer's court. It places you side by side working with them to solve their problems. This increases the likelihood of them calling on you when they are looking for a solution for a current project.

IRRITATION

Irritation is merely a small anger. Just as you can sense when somebody is irritated with you, be aware that people can sense when you are irritated with them. It's not just what you say that shows your irritation with others, but your body language as well will give you away. So, make sure that your irritations are kept "under wraps". As you grow toward wholeness and positive self-esteem, your control over your emotions will give you such a solid sense of self-worth that irritations will very seldom bother you.

IMAGINATION

"If one advances confidently in the direction
of his dreams, and endeavors to live the life which
he has imagined, he will meet with a success
unexpected in common hours."

Henry Thoreau

Einstein said, "Imagination is more powerful than knowledge."

HOW DO I RATE? HOW CAN I IMPROVE?

IDEAS_____

_____

IRRITATION_____

_____

IMAGINATION_____

_____

J

JOKES

While it is important to have a good sense of humor, a salesperson should be extremely cautious when telling jokes. Jokes can offend, especially those with an ethnic, sexist, or religious twist. The safest position on jokes is to refrain from telling them, unless you know the customer very well.

The old image of the backslapping, joke telling, loud-talking salesman is a thing of the past. Customers are now accustomed to dealing with salespeople who conduct themselves as the trained professionals they are.

In the past I would call on a customer who was a very spiritual man. One day I was calling on him with one of our regional managers from a company I represented. During the conversation over lunch, the regional manager decided to tell a very crude joke. Needless to say as the joke progressed I could watch my customer becoming very uncomfortable. As I witnessed his discomfort, I became uncomfortable as well. I tried to good-naturedly signal the regional manager, but he was on a roll and it would have been very difficult to stop him at that time. The relationship I had with the customer was not greatly affected, but the relationship between the customer and the regional manager's company was somewhat damaged.

Be very careful, then, if you decide to tell jokes. Be sure they're both truly humorous and inoffensive to your intended audience.

JUGGLING

Utilize your time according to Pareto's Principle, also known as the 80/20 rule. Eighty percent of your sales come from twenty percent of your customers. Eighty percent of your profits come from twenty percent of your products. Schedule your time accordingly.

Using time wisely is as important as being industrious. (See also **TIME** and **ORGANIZATION**.)

When first entering sales, there is a tendency to spend more time with those customers whom you like and not necessarily with those who buy the most. You must learn to define the customers with the greatest buying potential and then spend a disproportionate part of your time in soliciting their business. Whether or not you're particularly comfortable with them is of little consequence. You need to allot your time to those areas that have the greatest potential for you in total sales.

HOW DO I RATE? HOW CAN I IMPROVE?

JOKES_____

_____

JUGGLING_____

_____

K

KICKBACKS

At some time during your sales career, you will probably be offered a kickback.

Don't take it. Kickbacks create resentment. Kickbacks do not establish a professional sales relationship. Kickbacks are illegal.

An example of a kickback is when you pay the buyer for doing business with you. All you have to do is get caught once and even if you don't go to jail, your reputation will be ruined.

In sales, your reputation is paramount. As soon as the word is out on the street that you have been paying kickbacks your name and good reputation will never be the same. The opportunity to remain in a sales position will be greatly reduced. People throughout the industry will know of your dealings and will be turned off when you call on them.

Imagine how you would feel to have your friends, family, children, members of your community, your profession, and your industry know that you have been paying kickbacks to get business. For years one of my competitors established his customer base by paying people to buy his product. He would kickback part of his commission to the buyer for buying from him. He is currently under indictment and will in all likelihood go to prison. What goes around comes around. Even if you escape prosecution, in the final analysis you still have to live with yourself. Your loss of personal integrity is probably the greatest form of punishment.

KINDNESS

Kindness should be a lifestyle.

"The world is not changed by great deeds, but rather by random acts of kindness. "

Mother Teresa

KINGS

Remember, it's always better to be a king maker than a king. Your customer is a king, as is your sales manager. Your job is to make their jobs easier.

Robert Greenleaf writes about this in his book, *Servant Leadership.* You learn how to truly lead by thinking like a servant.

Becoming a king should not be your goal, for in that obsession you will lose sight of your real goal. Peers become suspicious and jealous of others attempting to set themselves up as kings. Rather than support your efforts, they will sabotage you.

HOW DO I RATE? HOW CAN I IMPROVE?

KICKBACKS_____

_____

KINDNESS_____

_____

KINGS_____

_____

LAZINESS

Laziness is often the downfall of the new salesman. A sales career does provide a great deal of freedom. The temptation to play instead of work can be great (see also **DISCIPLINE**).

In many fields and industries, sales can be a numbers game. If you call on twenty people a week and close twenty percent of those calls, you will make four sales a week. If you double the number of calls, you will double your number of sales per week. How many sales calls are you willing to make in a week?

In addition to the number of sales that you make, the amount of energy that you put into each sales call will also make a difference. Since most people tend to be lazy and try to get by with the minimum effort, your energy and maximum effort will pay off.

One way to use laziness to your advantage is to encourage it in your customer. Do as much of the customer's work for him as possible. The easier you make his job, and the more dependent you make him on you, the more you will benefit. Your sales relationship will become more secure.

There is a natural tendency to become complacent once you have achieved some success, established a good customer base and improved your business. I know, it happened to me.

After some fifteen years in sales, I became complacent. As the day follows the night, laziness follows complacency. I became lazy. I wasn't putting the same number of hours in each week. I wasn't working as hard. Gradually, I noticed my sales dipping and my competitors moving into a stronger position in my territory. I went through all the justifications: our prices had gone up, our competitors were working harder, the quality of their products was catching up with our products.

Were those the real reasons why I was losing sales? In the final analysis, I had become complacent thinking that I was going to get the business regardless of my effort – or lack of effort. I had met the enemy and it was me.

LISTENING

Listening skills are probably the single most important skill to master for the professional salesman today.

Selling is basically a matter of matching products to needs. The way to discover your customer's needs is to listen. Learn to listen with your ears, your eyes, and your instincts.

The communication circle is not complete unless the other person understands your message and you understand theirs. Your job as a salesperson depends greatly on making sure that this circle of communication and understanding on the part of both the customer and yourself is complete. Make sure that you are receiving the message your customer is sending. Ask questions and go back over the conversation until you are both clear.

Watch your customer's body language, especially the facial expressions, to determine whether or not they are getting your message. It not, go back over and see if any points need clarification. As a salesperson, one of the most beneficial things you could do for yourself is to seek out a good course in listening skills. These are available through tapes, books, and seminars.

Utilize the 80/20 rule where you talk 20 percent of the time and listen 80 percent. The 20 percent talking should be used primarily to ask the correct questions to clarify your customer's needs and then tailor your presentation accordingly.

LOSING

In your sales career you will win some and lose some. When I lose potential business I have found that nine out of ten times, it's because I was outsold – not because the customer was being paid off or got a cheaper price from my competitor, or some other excuse I dreamed up.

More often than not the customer had a better relationship with my competition and felt more comfortable with their products than they did with mine. The best thing for a sales professional to do when he "loses" is to avoid a negative reaction and use the situation to his advantage instead.

The professional salesman uses the loss as an educational tool. Review objectively what you did or did not do that cost you the order. This process will prevent you from making the same mistake in the future. I suggest making an appointment with the customer to find out why you lost the sale and learn how you can do your job better next time.

It has always amazed me that I learn more from my losses than I do from my successes. When I lose and investigate the causes, I gain invaluable information on how to win in the future.

Learn to lose with grace. When the final decision has been made to award the business to your competitor, meet with your customer and simply say how much you appreciated their time and the opportunity to present your ideas, products or services. You may even want to ask them what you could possibly do next time to enhance your opportunity.

Several years ago I called on a customer concerning the potential of using one of the pumps that I sold. The customer was unfamiliar with the pump, and as comfortable as I tried to make him feel explaining the technical advantages of using our pump, he still could not come to a comfort level. I called the pump manufacturer and the president of the company. I made a call on the plant and offered him the opportunity of using one of our pumps for an undetermined period of time to see if he could become more comfortable with it. He installed it alongside the competitive pumps he had been using, and we let him demo the pump for approximately six months. After that period of time, he was satisfied that our pump was the right pump for him. The engineer who was designing the job was satisfied that ours was the right pump. We eventually bid against our competitor's pump.

We were a little bit high on capital cost and it went into evaluation. Again, I talked with my customer with whom we had left the pump, and he was in favor of using our pump. He even went out and visited a job site and talked to a customer who had been using our pump for a number of years. This solidified his position on using our equipment even more strongly. I talked to the engineer and he said it looked like a go and they were in the final throes of making the decision.

To my amazement and complete surprise they went with my competitor. After having been told by the customer, the engineer, and the customer's project manager that they had all agreed on our pump for that particular job, the deal fell through.

Investigating afterwards as to why they made the decision to go with my competitor, I discovered that the man who was in charge of plant maintenance was concerned about his unfamiliarity with our pump. Since he had been using my competitor's pump for a number of years, he had a higher degree of familiarity and comfort with it. His opinion carried enough weight and influence that it swayed the decision over to my competitor.

I learned, as I discussed in the section titled **DECISION MAKER**, that I had not covered all the bases. Had I known that this employee was part of the decision making process, I would have gone to him early on, met with him, and found out directly if he had any concerns. I would have found out what his needs were, and would have tried to develop a comfort level with him as well. Perhaps in this particular case I would have been successful if I had covered all the decision-makers. Since I had not done that, I lost the order.

It was a very expensive lesson for me to learn but I learned it well. It emphasized to me once again that I must cover every buying influence on every job so as to minimize my risk of loss.

LUCK

Most people think of luck as winning the Lotto. In business, if you work hard enough and long enough you will make your own luck. If you leave your chances up to luck you will come up short every time. It is hard work, persistence, and maximum effort that pay off in rewards, not luck.

Bobby Dodd said it best: **"Luck is when preparation meets opportunity."**

HOW DO I RATE? HOW CAN I IMPROVE?

LAZINESS_____

_____

LISTENING_____

_____

LOSING_____

_____

LUCK_____

_____

M

MAYBE

When a customer says "maybe" it could mean several different things:

- ◆ They are beginning to consider your point of view.

- ◆ They don't necessarily agree with what you said.

- ◆ They have some doubts left concerning your product.

- ◆ You are not even close to making the sale.

- ◆ You are off track.

The word "maybe" is a signal for you to stop talking and start asking questions to discover the problem.

MENTORS

When you first start your sales career, look around for successful people – in your company in particular and in the sales field in general. Look for the people who are the sales leaders in your industry. Look for the people who are the leaders in your own firm.

Once you have identified the winners, study them carefully and discover what makes them successful. Ask the individuals themselves, if possible. Ask anyone who could give you insight into the secrets of the winner's success.

Once you identify patterns or methods, apply these skills to your own work methods. You need not slavishly copy the leaders, however. You will benefit from taking from them that which is likely to work for you, and that which fits with your own personal style. This mentor approach can minimize the painful trial and error method of developing successful skills. Emulating what has already proved successful in the field can also save you valuable time.

Several years ago I was invited to a dinner party consisting of eight couples, all husbands and wives. Part of the evening was spent in a game where each couple would write down who they believed were their spouses' three favorite heroes. My wife was right on the money with Will Rogers, Vince Lombardi, and Winston Churchill. Identifying your own heroes will tell you a lot about yourself. All three of these men had strong convictions, a good sense of humor, and a great deal of courage and faith. All three of them had a strong following because of the kind of people they were. All three had the courage of their convictions in their field of endeavor and were extremely successful men.

It is a valuable lesson to read about the lives of great men because it will give you insights and clues into how to lead your own life. If you look at the makeup of most of the great people in history, you will see that they share a great many of the same values.

MIND

We become what we think. Man has the power to choose who he becomes. Your actions and choices in life develop your character. Thinking positively works to your advantage. Being goal-oriented directs our efforts toward positive outcomes.

The mind, like a computer, can be programmed. You are in charge of the input, so don't waste your time with negative programming. The GIGO principle (garbage in, garbage out) doesn't just apply to computers.

The mind might be compared as well to a movie projector, with your whole life as the screen on which your particular movie is projected. If you see the world in a negative light, one that is fearful, full of suspicions, danger, and sadness, then you should look inside yourself.

You are projecting from within. You need to change reels, to one that portrays positive attitudes and actions. This book, if followed, will give you the tools to become positive in your outlook by building success upon success. It is always amazing to me how the outside world changes when I change what is going on inside. We see the world not as it is, but as we are.

All in the State of Mind

If you think you're beaten, you are

If you think you dare not, you don't

If you'd like to win, but think you can't

It's almost a cinch you won't

If you think you'll lose, you're lost.

For out in the world you'll find

Success begins with a fellow's will.

It's all in the state of mind.

For many a game is lost

'Ere ever a step is run; And many a coward fails

'Ere ever his work's begun.

Think big, and your deeds will grow;

Think small, and you'll fall behind;

Think that you can, and you will.

It's all in the state of mind.

If you think you're outclassed, you are;

You've got to think high to rise.

You've got to be sure of yourself before

You can ever win a Prize.

Life's battles don't always go

To the stronger or faster man.

But soon or late the man who wins

Is the fellow who thinks he can.

-ANON

MISTAKES

Remove the word *mistake* from your vocabulary. It is another one of those words with negative connotations.

Take the attitude that mistakes are just missed opportunities. Look at them in a favorable light with the understanding that you can use them as stepping-stones to success.

You will be amazed how productive attitudes and dealing constructively with co-workers about missed opportunities (rather than criticizing them for making mistakes) leads to further growth. People will learn from their mistakes when they are handled in a positive manner. Never criticize yourself for your own mistakes, since you will simply reinforce them and set yourself up to make more errors.

MONEY

Don't make money your ultimate goal.   Rather, pray for the freedom from worry over money.

MUST

Must is a word of command, which often puts the listener on the defensive and which may be considered insulting.   Put yourself on the other side of the desk, in your customer's chair, and listen to these statements: "You *must* buy this product." "You *must* listen to reason." "You *must* understand what I'm saying."   No one *must* do anything – especially if they're doing the buying.

HOW DO I RATE? HOW CAN I IMPROVE?

MAYBE_____

_____

MENTORS_____

_____

MIND_____

_____

MISTAKES_____

_____

MUST_____

_____

N

NAMES

People love to hear their own names. Our names are something of which we are all proud. People with positive self-images will always offer their names first when meeting other people. It is very important to remember the names of those people you will be in contact with in the business world, and TO use them.

NEEDS

The basic process of selling is assessing a customer's needs, and matching the best possible product to meet these needs. The most important part of your sales call will be asking the right questions to discover the exact needs, expectations and requirements of your customer.

Once you discover the customer's basic needs and requirements, other needs of theirs may still potentially interfere with the sale. Do they need a better delivery date? Do they need a better price? Do they need more assurance that your product will fulfill their needs? Do they need to know more about the technical merits of your product? Do they need to know more about your company? Do they need to know more about how your product will satisfy their own customer's needs, or do they simply need to know that you want to do business with them?

The professional salesman is constantly aware of their customer's needs before, during, and after the sale. Successful salesmen do whatever they must to make sure that these needs are met.

NERVOUSNESS

When you are just beginning a sales career minor nervousness is okay and, in fact, is often expected by the customer. If nervousness persists you can learn to use meditation to overcome nerves.

Sit in a relaxed position. Close your eyes, breathe deeply four or five times, focusing on the intake and exhaling of your breath. Then allow a picture of a peaceful scene in nature – sitting on the beach, lying in a meadow under a sky filled with slowly moving fluffy clouds – to fill your mind's eye. Enjoy the sensations of being in this special place with all your senses.

When thoughts come into your mind simply let them pass on through. Don't focus on them. Repeat the word "One" over and over to yourself. Repeat this exercise each morning and each evening. It will help you take control of your nerves.

As mentioned under **VISUALIZATION,** it will help to go over each sales call in your mind prior to the call, planning each step and projecting a positive outcome.

If, however, you continue to be nervous in a sales situation, your nervousness will cause the customer to become uneasy. Continued nervousness with clients requires analysis to discover what the cause is. Often it is just a matter of making simple adjustments in your thinking, changing negative thoughts to positive ones. Coaches, consultants or counselors can help you make these simple but important changes quickly and easily.

NEVER

Never is another of those negative words that you will want to eliminate from your sales vocabulary. There is an old adage: "Never say never."

NO

There is another old saying that when a customer says "No" the sale really begins. There is a tendency for new salespeople to automatically accept "No" as final. The experienced salesperson, however, knows that "No" is rarely final.

The customer's refusal may mean that they are just not ready to buy at this time. It may mean that they are still not convinced that your products or services are what they need. It may mean that they still have some additional concerns about your products and that, if these concerns could be alleviated, the sale could be concluded.

Your sales manager can demonstrate probing questions that you might use to get behind the customer's "No" in a tactful, non-aggressive way.

NON-RESISTANCE

Too many times when a salesman is pointing out the advantages of their product, the customer throws up an objection to the advantage, and we meet this objection with resistance. Recognize and allow for the value in his objection, and so state. For example: "I see the value in what you're saying, but let me point out..." Then, go on to offer the feature of your product that would overcome that objection.

If you meet their objection with resistance and try to discredit it, you will automatically put them in an adversarial role. You will end up putting the customer on the defensive, and they will then resist your attempt to demonstrate the feature or functions of your product that would meet and overcome their objection.

So, the idea of non-resistance is to set up an atmosphere between you and the customer where neither is resisting the ideas of the other. So many times when a young salesman hears an objection voiced to their concepts, products, or services, they immediately try to prove the customer's statement wrong. This sets up a debate between you and the customer rather than developing a mutual ground of respect.

You never want to get into a debate with your customer, because I can promise you that the salesman will lose these debates *one hundred percent of the time.*

NOW

Positive, professional salespeople live in the *now.* They do not worry about the past, especially past mistakes. They are not concerned with the future, especially the ills that the future might bring.

The successful professional salesman pays attention to what is happening right now. They do those things today that will make them a better salesman. They do those things today that will develop stronger relationships with clients and customers. They do those things today that will move them towards the close of a sale.

The positive and successful sales professional knows that in reality, today is all they have, and strives to make the best of each moment of each day. They have a firm, personal mission for themselves, which leaves no room for worrying about the past or the future. They put their energy into now knowing that what is done today will create a successful future.

Make a list of things you must accomplish today and assign priority to the most important ones. Start on these immediately, even if it is not pleasant. In fact, getting the most onerous tasks out of the way first will give you a sense of accomplishment and speed you on your way.

When focusing on the now, you can monitor the thoughts that come into your head. You can monitor the food that goes into your body. You can monitor the exercise for physical fitness you choose to perform that day. You can monitor your alcohol or tobacco consumption. You can choose, in short, to do or not do anything, in the moment.

Successful people eliminate negative actions and thoughts by focusing on the moment and making positive choices *now*. People who are constantly worried about the past and fearful of the future become frozen in their emotions, and they forget how to live.

By living in the now, life becomes less complicated. By living in the now and living this moment as it comes, life becomes more enjoyable because you control the way you choose to spend the moments of your day. Living in the now, you become more alive.

NUTRITION

Proper nutrition is essential for physical and mental fitness, since it is the fuel that provides energy for the body and the brain. Just as cheap fuel for your car will make the engine ping and sputter, not paying attention to what we eat results in poor nutrition and reduced performance. The results are fatigue in the short run and disease in the long run.

For effectively feeding your body, a simple rule to follow is:

◆ For breakfast, eat like a king.

This is the most important meal of the day. You need to have protein to provide adequate fuel for the bulk of the day's activities. Your body can assimilate 20 grams of protein in the morning. A breakfast of cereal, milk and toast may not provide all the protein you need.

◆ For lunch, eat like a queen.

Additional protein can be consumed for lunch, but limit yourself again to 20 grams, which is approximately three ounces of meat. A ham and cheese sandwich provides 20 grams of protein.

◆ For dinner, eat like a peasant.

   Vegetables, soup, baked potatoes, pasta and salads can easily be digested overnight. Eat early and eat lightly. Red meat consumed at night does not digest well, and the longer it stays in the system at rest, the greater chance that it will be converted to fat.

◆ Between meals, eat fruit for snacks.

◆ During the day drink at least eight 8-oz glasses of water.

These are merely suggested guidelines. You should consult your physician and a nutritionist for more in-depth recommendations to the above.

HOW DO I RATE? HOW CAN I IMPROVE?

NAME_____

_____

NEEDS_____

_____

NERVOUSNESS_____

_____

NEVER_____

_____

NO_____

_____

NON-RESISTANCE_____

_____

NOW_____

_____

OBJECTIONS

When a customer shows a concern or an objection about your product, they are telling you that they are not ready to buy from you at this point. Your job as a salesman is to learn what their concerns or objections really are in order to determine whether or not they are indeed legitimate concerns, and then try to overcome them.

Individual companies generally offer sales training to enable the new salesman to overcome customer objections, but one rule of thumb is to repeat their objection verbally to make sure you do understand it. Simply say, "What I heard you say was_____. Is that correct?"

Remember, however, that the stated objection is often not the real objection. Successful salesmen learn to listen, and read, between the lines. Asking questions and then *listening* to the answers is the best way to uncover objections so you can overcome them.

OBSTACLES

Do you avoid obstacles, or go around them? Do you meet obstacles head-on and work your way through them?

Successful salesmen meet obstacles as they arise and work their way through them to a positive conclusion. A successful attitude toward obstacles is that they create opportunities to actually move closer to obtaining the order.

The salesman who avoids obstacles and tends to walk around them rather than face them loses many business opportunities. This individual walks away from many sales prematurely. Additionally, they lose creditability in the marketplace and can wind up with a reputation as someone not willing to go the extra mile. Customers and clients value the people who can solve their problems. Consider meeting obstacles head-on a way of proving your value to your client.

You can only overcome obstacles by working your way through them. If you continually try to avoid or go around them, they will end up overtaking you down the road. Obstacles taken care of early in the business relationship and handled in a positive fashion don't create future problems. Most obstacles that you avoid or try to go around today can grow into bigger problems tomorrow – and eventually become insurmountable.

ORGANIZATION

Organizing yourself is a key factor in minimizing mistakes and maximizing opportunities. Time management experts tell us that one hour spent in planning each week saves a minimum of two hours per day, so plan ahead.

Have the right equipment. Purchase a PDA, a Blackberry, or both a desk and pocket calendar, and commit to using them effectively. Update your cellphone listings. Deal with your email in a timely fashion.

Organization includes maintaining a file system of information, electronic or otherwise. I suggest keeping a file on each customer or project that you call or work on. Keep these files accessible (today, that can include laptop accessibility) when you call on customers. Review your notes prior to meeting with clients. Your customer will be impressed that you remembered what was covered in your last meeting. They will be even more impressed if you have handled what was promised previously. Since you entered this in your database, taking care of what was promised became a simple and easy task.

Your customer will appreciate your organization and the time that it saves you both.

Organize your time so that you fill each day with activities that will enable you to do business, keep business, and maximize your opportunities for success.

HOW DO I RATE? HOW CAN I IMPROVE?

OBJECTIONS_____

_____

OBSTACLES_____

_____

ORGANIZATION_____

_____

P

PERSISTENCE

"Nothing in the world can take the place of persistence. Talent will not; nothing is more common than unsuccessful men with talent. Genius will not; unrewarded genius is almost a proverb. Education will not; the world is full of educated derelicts. Persistence and determination alone are omnipotent."

Calvin Coolidge

Denis Waitley offers the following statistics from the National Sales Executive Association: Eighty percent of all new sales are made after the fifth call. Forty percent of the salesmen make only one call and quit. Twenty-five percent make two calls and quit. Twelve percent make three calls and quit. Only ten percent of the salespeople keep calling, and they are the highest-paid people in the world. It's the ten percent who persist who get the payoff.

You should also learn to recognize when you have gone far enough and it is time to back off. A point is reached in each sales opportunity where the final decision has already been made to buy from your competitor. It is at this point you should know how to bow out gracefully.

I have been in situations where I have had all the cards in my favor – price, quality, and better delivery – but the customer still favored my competitor. When I finally asked why, the customer told me he was unfamiliar with my product and he didn't have enough time on this project to evaluate it fairly. He had been using my competitor's product and was comfortable with it. I told him that I understood and I would work with him in the future to gain his confidence in our product. There was no way at that time that I was going to change his mind, and I recognized this. Had I persisted, not only would I have lost his order, I could also have jeopardized any future opportunities.

PERSONALITIES

In sales, as in life, you will encounter a number of different personality types. Some suggest that there are nine basic personality types ranging from the introvert to a Hitler type. Making a study of personality types is essential in sales in order to understand what motivates people and thus be able to interact successfully with them. One way you can do this is by understanding the different personality types that you'll come across in everyday life. One should try to understand their motivations, their fears, and their personal needs. By doing so you will be far ahead of the game.

By nature I am aggressive and there are many people I might offend if I did not control my aggression. Some people want to be pushed, others want to be pulled along, while others just want to have all the facts and make a decision for themselves. It is important to know with whom you are dealing.

If you try to aggressively push someone into a decision when they prefer to make the decision for themselves, you may end up pushing them in the direction of your competitor. I'm suggesting that you learn the psychology of personality types in order to give you the ability to work with different types of people. There are personalities with whom you're comfortable and others that turn you off. I'm not suggesting you become a chameleon and adapt your own personality to each person you encounter. By recognizing the different types, however, you will get comfortable and learn to successfully interact with them all.

Let's examine these nine different personalities that you will likely come in contact with in your day-to-day selling. (These are adapted from Richard Riso's *Personality Types*).

1. ***The School Teacher.*** This individual wants to be actively involved in how you do your job. Let them, it will involve them with you and that's the best you can ask for. If you fight their need to teach you they will find someone else who will listen. Ask them for their advice and opinions. You will not only learn something, but you will be appealing to their basic instincts to share their wisdom. School teacher types are also often preoccupied with perfection, so make sure you handle even the smallest of details with care when dealing with them.

2. ***The Caretaker.*** These people want to control you, tell you how to sell, and how to live your life. Don't take offense, as this is their nature. Let them think they are in control.

3. ***The Ambitious One.*** These persons strive to be the best they can be. They like to be winners and to surround themselves with winners. They are upwardly mobile and want to be liked. Show how you can be helpful and can assist them in moving up if they work with you.

4. ***The Artist.*** Creative, introverted, and individualistic. Be creative yourself, show them different and new ideas on how your products or services can be used.

5. ***The Thinker.*** Perceptive and analytical, these individuals like to observe, are naturally curious and prefer to gather a lot of data before making a decision. You need to be able to supply reams of data to the Thinker that will support him or her in moving toward your product. You can't push them into a decision. You need to be able to provide a great deal of information and effectively communicate the merits of it to them.

6. ***The Loyalist.*** Likable, dutiful and dependable, this is your quintessential "company man" or woman. They are not so interested in how your product or service will help them, but in how it will be of benefit to their company.

7. ***The Fun Seeker.*** Excitable, enthusiastic, and extroverted, the Fun Seeker responds to excitement and the wonders of life. These people respond to being entertained and enjoy being around enthusiastic, upbeat people. You can accomplish more with them on the golf course than within the confines of their office.

8. ***The Leader.*** Self-confident and powerful, possibly dictatorial, Leader types can be overbearing and come across as Attila the Hun. Often, inside them is a Teddy Bear personality. You don't want to confront them directly when they are coming on too strong, but you don't want to be run over, either. Don't back down from your position if they attack you or your product. By responding to their strong-arm tactics with kindness and understanding rather than anger, you show them that you recognize their position. You diffuse them. Ultimately they will respect you for the way you handle yourself. Since they are always involved in championing the people they have a relationship with, you will find you have a powerful ally if you make your cause their cause.

9. ***The Peacemaker.*** The Peacemaker is passive, kind, patient, and gentle. They can tend to be lazy and let others take charge. You can become a real asset to them by making their job easier. Help them in their decision making to move away from the tendency to procrastinate. Push them – but gently.

During my first job as a sales manager I had occasion to call on a potential customer with one of our salesmen. The customer we were calling on was one of the largest fruit gift shippers in Florida, and he had a brochure that he mailed out throughout the United States. It was a beautiful multicolored brochure showing the oranges and the rest of the fruit that his company packed and shipped. He used this brochure as a sales tool.

The company that I was working for was in the printing business. When I initially called him to set up an appointment I could tell that he wasn't exactly excited to see us. When we actually got there and were seated in his office, I began my pitch. He quickly let me know that he had viewed the printing our company put out, and there was no way that we could produce the quality he insisted on from his printer in Atlanta. He told us he appreciated our coming up to see him but that it was probably a wasted trip because he was satisfied with his current printer.

I agreed with him that, in the past, we had primarily been a black and white printer of forms but we had recently purchased a four-color press, and were doing some excellent color work. I asked him if he would mind on our next call if we brought some of our magazines and brochures to show him the level of quality we were now producing.

Grudgingly, he agreed to our coming again in the future. As we walked out of the building the other salesman looked at me and said

"Are you crazy? That man no more wants to do business with us than the man in the moon!" He thought the man was rude, so why should we waste our time coming back to see someone who will treat us in that manner?

I said, "First, he has a great deal of potential business. Secondly, he has not seen the quality of work we are currently doing; and finally, once he sees it we might convince him to do business locally rather than out of state." I suggested we plan another trip in a couple of weeks, bringing along a copy of the golf magazine and the multicolored tourist brochures we were now producing. When we returned we would try to convince him that we were the right firm to have his business.

To make a long story short, when we did go back to visit the packing company owner he found that our products not only met but exceeded the quality he was receiving from the Atlanta firm. Our proposal was higher than his current printer, but he was satisfied that the level of our quality was sufficient that paying the difference was justified.

There is a great lesson to be learned from this. So many times when we are treated rudely and abruptly in sales we take it personally. We must realize that when people are rude, gruff, and abrupt, it is not us they are upset with. They may have a whole different agenda. It may simply be part of their personality, the way they carry and conduct themselves. It may also be that they have had a rough time of it lately and are taking some of that out on the next person through the door. If you view people in that light you will not take offense by the way they conduct themselves. Whenever you get defensive, you simply establish an adversary role.

Give people time to bring themselves back into line, so that a potentially satisfactory relationship can develop. Frequently when we are out in the territory for the first time, calling on people with whom we have not yet established a relationship, we may react negatively to them. If they are uptight, anxious, antagonistic, or nervous we commonly assume that the fault must lie with us. The trick is to understand that it is not personal. When we understand different personalities and how they function, we can let go of defensiveness, relax, and be ourselves.

By becoming familiar with the different personality types as well as understanding your own, you will come to have a healthy respect for each individual's personality, the extrovert as well as the introvert, the more passive person as well as the aggressor. Demonstrate that respect, and you will have come a long way in building good relationships.

PREPARATION

"If you fail to prepare, you are preparing to fail." A successful life has to include preparation in every arena. We have talked all through this book about preparing yourself mentally, physically, spiritually, and emotionally.   Nothing can be accomplished to ultimate satisfaction without proper preparation.   When it comes down to two equally matched opponents, the victory usually goes to the one that is best prepared.

Some will read this book, put it down, and forget it. Others will read it and use it as a tool for success.   They will put into practice what they have learned, using the book as a reference and a stepping stone to branch out and delve more deeply into other resources.

PRICE

There will always be someone who builds his product a little worse, so he can sell it cheaper.   And those who buy on price alone are this man's lawful prey.

PURCHASING AGENTS

Old timers in the sales field may imply that a purchasing agent is concerned only with the bottom line pricing, and takes nothing else into consideration.   This may have been true in the past;   however, purchasing agents today are often highly trained, professional decision-makers.   You will want to treat professional purchasing agents with the same respect that you show any other customer, discovering their needs and demonstrating how your product can fulfill these needs.

Today's purchasing agent is concerned with more than just price.

As we discussed earlier, they're concerned with evaluated pricing that encompasses the total cost of doing business, not just the initial capital investment. They look at the maintenance cost that is required on the equipment, the energy cost required to run the equipment, and the projected cost of spare parts. They evaluate all these factors over a twenty-year product life cycle in order to compare one product versus another, rather than just looking at price as the sole determining factor.

It's important to know the total evaluated cost of your products so you can present them that way, as opposed to selling just on low price. If price is the only thing you can sell, you will never make it as a professional salesman and you will end up working for mediocre companies that sometimes have a short-lived existence in the marketplace. You want to sell for a company whose philosophy encompasses everything we've discussed and whose product offers a total value to the customer. Then you will be selling on a truly professional level.

HOW DO I RATE? HOW CAN I IMPROVE?

PERSISTENCE_____

_____

PERSONALITIES_____

_____

PREPARATION_____

_____

PURCHASING AGENTS_____

_____

QUALITY

Quality is more than just your goods and services. Quality is measured by the total package: you, your product, your presentation of products and services, the relationship that you establish with your customer, your reputation in the industry, and your integrity. Remember, people buy from people they like and trust. It is important to monitor the quality of your total package and work toward excellence in all of these areas.

QUESTIONS

In selling, the purpose of asking questions is to encourage the customer to talk. If the customer never talks, you never find out what they really want and what their real needs are.

Practice asking questions in a non-offensive, non-aggressive manner, and make it clear to your customer that you do want to learn exactly what their needs are. Listen carefully to your customer's answers. The information you gather will give you insight as to how best present your products, goods, or services. A good rule of thumb is to use 80 percent of your sales call in listening and 20 percent of talking. And, most of your 20 percent should come in the form of *questions*.

The only way to discover the real needs of a customer is to ask probing questions, then listen carefully to the answers so you can present your product or services in a light that meets his needs. The following is a list of typical questions:

1. How important is the initial capital cost of the product?

2. How important is the energy cost of the product?

3. How important is the operation and maintenance cost of the product?

4. How important is fast delivery? Are you in constant crisis for this product, or do you have long lead times available to you?

5. How important is the local warehousing of spare parts, or do you normally have more than twenty-four hours leeway once you have something break down?

6. How important to you is the availability of local service? Do you need a serviceman available to service your equipment within twenty-four hours notice?

7. What standard of quality do you need in the product?

8. How important is the safety of the product?

9. How important is technical assistance to you in laying out the total design?

By understanding and asking the proper questions you can tailor your sales pitch exactly to the customer's concerns, wants, and needs. Avoid a canned sales pitch; don't just walk in there with a fifteen-minute dialog of how great your product is. It is guaranteed to bore them to tears.

After calling on a particular customer for a while, once you are past the early stages of establishing a relationship, ask questions which will allow you to know more about them as a person. Ask them more personal questions such as where they are from, are they married, how many children do they have, what are their ages and what are they involved in. Get to know their desires within the company, and their goals, asking where they would like to be five years down the road. Find out about their community background, their social life, sports or hobbies, where they went to college, and what their affiliations are.

As you get to know the total person you learn to accept them more as a human being than as just a customer. You will normally find that you have some levels of commonality that will help you to establish a personal relationship with the potential customer, as well as establishing a long-lasting business relationship.

QUIET

Each day try to spend some quiet time alone in a pleasant setting, keeping company with yourself and your own thoughts. Use this time to reflect on where you are. Collect your thoughts while removed from the hustle and bustle of the day, and review what you have accomplished today. Focus on where you are headed with your life and your career.

QUOTAS

When you first go into sales, especially if you are working for a very large company, you will be given a territory with established quotas for that territory. It is very important when establishing quotas that you be involved in the makeup of what that quota is to be.

Be sure that you question your sales manager in order to understand where and how the quota was established, so that you will have confidence in it. There is nothing more discouraging than having an unrealistic sales quota, which causes you to continually bang your head up against a number that realistically you will never be able to meet.

This happens more often than one would care to think, because inexperienced sales managers may establish unrealistic quotas in order to make themselves look good. After being in the territory for half a year to a year, you will have a better feel for what your quota should be, so that the next year's quota will be established in concert with the sales manager of the company. This number will probably be more reflective of what can really be expected out of the territory because you will then have a feel for what that territory can actually produce. Having been part and parcel in establishing that quota, you will have confidence in it and you will be motivated not only to try and meet the quota, but to exceed it.

Hopefully, you work for a company that will allow you to profit from exceeding quotas; they might pay you an additional bonus to exceed the established quota. It is very important when you are initially interviewing companies to clearly understand the commission structure, the quotas and how they are established, and whether there is a realistic opportunity to make money, and more money for more effort. Once again, remember we are talking about selling as a professional. Professional salesmen should be paid commensurate with their ability.

By being equally concerned about your customer's quotas and successes, your own quotas will take care of themselves.

HOW DO I RATE? HOW CAN I IMPROVE?

QUALITY_____

_____

QUESTIONS_____

_____

QUIET_____

_____

QUOTAS_____

_____

R

RECORDING IDEAS

I suggest keeping a recording device handy at all times. Most salespeople travel a large portion of the time. I have found that I get many ideas while driving or flying. The safest, easiest way for me to record these ideas is to record them on the spot to be transcribed later.

Many of the details that contribute to my success come to me as thoughts that drift in as I travel. By recording these thoughts, I become more efficient and effective in my territory. After my assistant has transcribed my thoughts – which include ideas on what follow up I need to do for the customer I just called on, products I need to check on, delivery dates, customer's needs, and general ideas on how to be more effective in my territory – I enter each item on my calendar and take action.

RELIABILITY

Reliability can be the key ingredient in forming a customer's buying decision. If the customer is weighing the different factors that come into play when determining purchase – price, service, and product integrity – and they all come out relatively even, intangibles come into play.

In reflecting on previous purchases, they will remember the salesman who was consistently *reliable.*

The customer will recall that when problems came up they were resolved in a professional and timely manner. They will remember who went to bat for them, and was willing to go the extra mile to make certain they were satisfied. It is the reliable salesman who usually ends up with the order.

This illustrates, once again, that the sale doesn't end with the purchase order. The true professional is the salesman who stays with the order until everyone is satisfied with the purchase.

REPETITION

Most boxing analysts agree that pound for pound, Sugar Ray Robinson was one of the greatest boxers who ever lived.

What made Sugar Ray great was the skills he developed in 3-4 combinations of hooks, uppercuts, and jabs. He worked on these combinations over and over again until they were honed to perfection. He didn't have to think to use them; they had become automatic.

The same approach can be applied to sales. If you take the values and concepts outlined in this book and use them repeatedly in your daily life, they will become a part of you. Your reputation will be developed through their application.

Just as Sugar Ray utilized his combinations to become a World Champion, you can become successful in your own right through repetition of the system given to you in these concepts.

RESPONSE TIME

The faster you respond to your customer's questions and/or problems, the faster you will build a solid relationship. If you allow small problems to remain unresolved, or do not respond to questions in a timely manner, the problems will grow. And, actually, the fact that you haven't responded promptly and appropriately will become a problem in itself.

RESPONSIBILITY

You need to learn to accept full responsibility for all of your actions. When you find you've made a mistake or the company has made a mistake or a product has failed, you should take responsibility for resolving the situation. Even if the mistake is not of your own making, once you start blaming other people the customer will lose confidence in you. You, after all, are the one they are really doing business with. In the final analysis they have chosen to do business with you for a number of reasons. If you start trying to deflect the blame to other areas, then they will have the opportunity to back away from doing business with you in the future.

So assume full responsibility for all that is under your control, and let the customer know in every situation that you are going to help them come up with the right solution.

The choice is up to you whether you choose to be successful or unsuccessful. The responsibility rests squarely on your shoulders and no one else's.

RETRIBUTION

When one loses, there is no room in the sales field for retribution or retaliation. Ideally, the professional salesman treats winning and losing the same way – recognizing both as potential stepping-stones to success.

Both winning and losing have much to teach. Value "losing" for its own unique lessons. Look for blame, if you must, only in reviewing the methods you used which did not work for you. Learn to use both winning and losing as indicators of what *does* work.

I have learned that ninety percent of my losses are directly related to my own efforts. And remember that being a "sore loser" makes other people uncomfortable. Since you may be attempting to do business with these same people in the future, it is best by far to leave a positive impression. In fact, your customer may so admire your behavior and your attitude that you will have the edge in the next round.

RIGHT

Learn to give up the need to be right. It is difficult to like someone who always, always has to be right. And remember, people buy from people they like. I once heard it said that we have two choices in life: We can choose to be right, or we can choose to be happy.

Remember, too, that the customer is not always right. When disputes arise, our job as a professional salesman is to determine what is fair for all parties involved and what is appropriate to each particular situation. Your job is to be a negotiator/arbitrator and to resolve difficult situations in a win/win manner, so that everyone walks away feeling that they have been treated fairly.

RISKS

"To laugh is to risk appearing the fool.

To weep is to risk appearing sentimental.

To reach out for another is to risk involvement.

To expose feelings is to risk exposing your true self.

To place your ideas, your dreams before the crowd is to risk their loss.

To love is to risk not being loved in return.

To live is to risk dying.

To hope is to risk despair.

To try is to risk failure.

But risks must be taken, because the greatest hazard in life is to risk nothing. The person who risks nothing, does nothing, has nothing and is nothing. He may avoid suffering and sorrow, but he simply cannot learn, feel, change, grow, love and live. Chained by his certitudes,

he is a slave, he has forfeited freedom.

Only a person who risks is free."

-Anonymous

RUDENESS

There is never any excuse to be rude to anyone. Remember, rudeness is not only conveyed by what you say. It can be transmitted with your eyes, gestures, and facial expressions. Be aware of how you carry yourself.

HOW DO I RATE? HOW CAN I IMPROVE?

RELIABILITY_____

_____

REPETITION_____

_____

RESPONSIBILITY_____

_____

RETRIBUTION_____

_____

RIGHT_____

_____

RISKS_____

_____

RUDENESS_____

_____

SECRETARY

Some of the most powerful and influential decision makers I have encountered in sales are the administrative assistants of my customers. Treat secretaries with respect, for they can often truly assist you in making the sale. I suggest that you make a rule for yourself to treat *everyone* in the company with equal respect. The manner in which you treat everyone you encounter in your customer's company is an indicator of your character. And, believe me, your customer will notice.

SELF-ESTEEM

If you believe, as I do, that we are largely responsible for our own success or failures in life, then why do some succeed while others lead lives of "quiet desperation?"

I believe self-esteem is the difference. Self-esteem can be achieved through positive self-development as outlined under Basic Training. Living your life as outlined in this book will bring you self-esteem, a solid foundation, and the joy of inner peace.

SELLING

Selling is a numbers game, and that is a simple cold hard fact. The more people you call on with the right message and the right product, competitively priced in a viable market, the more you will sell. By applying the values and concepts in this book you will be successful over and above the levels reached by those who just go out and call on sheer numbers of people.

This book outlines the attributes necessary to build a long-lasting, successful career, attributes such as treating others with respect and patience, conducting yourself according to your ethics and values, maintaining high motivation, and being persistent. These attributes all have one thing in common. They are under your control.

Highly successful people recognize those things that they have control over and utilize them; they also recognize those things that they can't control and don't waste their time banging their heads against walls. The choice is yours. You can play the numbers game and enjoy some degree of success, or apply these principles to your career and enjoy a rich and abundant life.

SERVICE AFTER THE SALE

No sale is completed until the product is installed, working properly, and all parties are satisfied. After your product has been sold and installed, there are likely to be problems from time to time. The way you handle these problems often determines your next sale and your continued, positive relationship with this customer.

Promptly respond to all telephone calls after the installation. Have a win/win philosophy so that all parties (both the customer and your company) feel that they have been treated fairly.

SIMPLIFY

Thoreau said **simplify, simplify, simplify**.   That was his approach to life.

The same philosophy can be applied in professional selling. You should try to make your approach to the marketplace as uncomplicated as possible and simplify your efforts to the point that you don't waste time and energy in unproductive areas.   In sales, proper use of your time is a key to success.

One suggestion is to take the time to make sure the customers you are calling on have the potential to buy the products you are offering.   There is no greater waste of time than to call on people with no need for your products.   You need to know your market to reduce wasted sales calls.

When I first went into sales my desk looked like a hamster cage, with bits and pieces of paper with phone calls and appointments strewn all over it.   When I arrived in the morning I would start wading through the paperwork with no real sense of direction. Invariably one of these pieces of paper would get lost and no action would be taken.   To combat this, I developed the following approach over the years.

I make a list at the beginning of each week, which includes everything I need to accomplish.   I prioritize the list based on importance and urgency.   During the week as additional things come up I add them to the existing list of items yet to be completed. This way I always have my agenda before me. It keeps me on top of things because everything I need to do is in one place. Very few items slip through the cracks.

We are the ones who make our lives too complex, which leads to anxiety and frustration because we try to use a system that is too intricate to follow.

Monitor your progress. Sit down once a month to see how you are measuring up against your goals. The concepts outlined in this book are, by intention, very basic. Simplicity pays off.

SKUNKS

Do not get into a spraying contest with a skunk; you will lose every time.

In every organization there will always be some disgruntled soul who is looking for someone upon which to dump his emotional garbage. Don't participate in this game, because his or her sole purpose is to transfer anger or emotional upsets over to you. When confronted with someone like this, simply say "I'm sorry you feel that way." This gives them back ownership of their feelings, and you don't walk away with them.

SMOKING

Over the past several years smoking has lost much of its appeal, witnessed by the millions of Americans who have given it up. Gone are the days of smoke-filled offices. If you smoke, smoke between appointments or when you are alone. Never light a cigarette in a customer's office. Even if the customer smokes, I recommend that you refrain from smoking during your sales call.

SPIRITUALITY

We were once spiritual beings in the universe, and we were given physical form through which to express our spirituality. Investigating and developing our own spiritual side enables us to grow as a person and to truly fulfill our potential.

STRESS

Stress is one of the major killers in the United States today. It can lead to heart disease, nervous breakdowns, ulcers, alcoholism, drug abuse and even death.

Below is a simple formula for a stress reduction plan that can lead to a high quality of life – and more of it:

S-top smoking.

T-rain for physical fitness four times a week.

R-elax through quiet time and meditation.

E-at properly by maintaining a diet of low fat, high fiber foods including vegetables, fish, and poultry, and drink a minimum of eight 8oz. glasses of water daily.

S-piritual life of positive values is invaluable.

S-erenity will be achieved by following the above.

STUDY

Know your product inside and out, from beginning to end. Know your competitor's product equally well. Know your industry. Know your territory.

Knowing your competitor's products, especially as it compares to yours, is often vital. Knowing your industry keeps you abreast of new developments. Knowing your customer and their company helps you match them with the product which best fits their needs.

SUCCESS

Many people define success as financial gain, power, prestige, recognition, or the accumulation of material goods. To me, success is doing what I love and loving what I do. Success is discovering my natural talents and using these in my life's work, to benefit both myself and my community. The result is that people who do what they love often do gain large sums of money, power, prestige and recognition.

If, however, you define success as material gain and power, you will ultimately find that there will never be such a thing as enough. The victory will be hollow, because material possessions alone do not make people lastingly happy.

HOW DO I RATE? HOW CAN I IMPROVE?

SECRETARY_____

_____

SELF-ESTEEM_____

_____

SELLING_____

_____

SERVICE AFTER THE SALE_____

_____

SIMPLIFY_____

_____

SKUNKS_____

_____

SMOKING_____

_____

SPOUSES_____

_____

STRESS_____

_____

STUDY_____

_____

SUCCESS_____

_____

T

TICKLER FILE

Another essential time management tool is a "tickler" calendar, whether simple or elaborate, to keep notes for follow-up. Whether on your computer, PDA, or desk calendar, entering things to do in the future under the appropriate date increases our efficiency, our reliability, and our effectiveness as a salesperson. When your customer's trust is at stake, it is best not to rely on your memory for dates and times of expected actions.

TIME

Positive utilization of your time is essential in developing your sales territory. Learning to prioritize ensures the most effective use of your time. Beginning with immediate needs of established customers, the next priority is to develop relationships with potential, "almost" customers – and so on down the line to cold calls.

Use the 80/20 rule to maximize your time to produce the best results in your territory. Eighty percent of your sales will come from twenty percent of your customers. Use this information to schedule the amount of time that you aim to spend with each customer. Practice identifying the established twenty percent in your territory as well as identifying potential customers to add to that twenty percent – and schedule your time accordingly.

Don't be fooled by the calendar. There are only as many days in the year as you make use of. One man gets only a week's value out of a year while another gets a full year's value out of a week.

Charles Richards

TRAVEL

Since time is a limited commodity, I find it beneficial to use my car travel time as productively as possible. Rather than listen to the radio or to music, I use my travel time for self-training and motivation. Many excellent CDs on sales skills, motivation, and self-help are available.

This book was dictated while on the road.

TRUST

One of the key ingredients in developing and maintaining a lasting, positive relationship with customers is mutual trust. Remember, people buy from people whom they like and trust. All decisions concerning your customer's needs should be made with this fact in mind. Never jeopardize the trust of your customer.

The best way to build mutual trust is to tell the truth, *always*, and to operate with a win/win philosophy. You want your customer to know that you are honest and that you are looking out for his interests. Once you have lost this trust, it is almost impossible to regain.

HOW DO I RATE? HOW CAN I IMPROVE?

TAPE RECORDER_____

_____

TICKLER FILE_____

_____

TIME_____

_____

TRAVEL/TIME_____

_____

TRUST_____

_____

U

UNIQUE

It is important to understand that every individual on the face of this earth is unique. Each of us has our own way of perceiving things and our own way of doing things. We have our own personalities and our own thoughts.

Learn to be comfortable with yourself and your uniqueness and you will be more accepting of the uniqueness of others. Take what you learn from this book, take what you learn from others, and incorporate only what truly fits your personality and your values. Develop your own approach; develop your own style.

Be yourself always, for when you are yourself and you are comfortable with yourself you will, in turn, make your customers comfortable.

HOW AM I UNIQUE? HOW CAN I BECOME EVEN MORE GENUINE?

_____

_____

_____

_____

V

VACATIONS

Taking a vacation at least twice a year is an absolute must in the stressful field of professional selling. You must have time away from the job, or the law of diminishing returns will set in and your productivity will drop. Your enthusiasm will eventually wear down and your motivation will decline. Eventually, your sales could drop off.

You need a vacation that is a non-working vacation. Do not take anything with you from the office to complete while on vacation. You need a complete break away from the business world. You need to put your mind to rest, and put your body at rest in a completely different setting and atmosphere from your job. The idea of a vacation is to recharge your batteries. It should not remind you of work.

My ideal vacation is one that I'm just about to take. My family and I have rented a cabin on a lake in North Carolina. I plan to go up there and sit on a dock by the lake and do absolutely nothing, other than a little boating, fishing, reading, and a lot of sleeping – nothing more strenuous than that.

VISUALIZATION

Your mind cannot distinguish between a real or imagined event. If you visualize successful outcomes to your selling efforts, you are more likely to achieve that result. Visualization is a process of positively rehearsing an event in your mind before its occurrence. Through visualization you will become less fearful. Rehearsing a positive outcome builds confidence, helps you relax and enables you to approach situations with a positive expectancy and attitude. You will begin to *act* in ways consistent with achieving desired outcomes.

Before making a sales call, try to visualize the entire meeting in your mind and address the following that will take place:

1. You are relaxed and confident as you enter the office.

2. The customer sitting at his desk greets you.

3. You make your delivery, asking about their needs.

4. Observe yourself handling any objections that arise.

5. Finally visualize a successful outcome to the meeting.

Preparing for each call in this manner will, over time, produce outstanding results.

HOW DO I RATE? HOW CAN I IMPROVE?

VACATIONS_____

_____

VISUALIZATION_____

_____

W

WINGS

As Frank Gorman, the astronaut, said when he was president of Eastern Airlines, "You have to earn your wings every day."

You can never sit back and rest on your laurels. You can never assume that you have it made, because as soon as you take a breath, your competition will be gaining on you from behind. So you have to go out there in the trenches everyday and give it 110 percent effort.

WINNING AND LOSING

I grew up in the 60's when we were taught that winning was everything. There were only two types of people, winners and losers, and there was no middle ground.

Vince Lombardi, the legendary coach, stated that winning wasn't everything; it was the only thing. Leo Durocher, the famous baseball manager, was quoted as saying, "You show me a good loser and I'll show you a loser."

That's the philosophy I grew up with. Starting football in the sixth grade and playing on through college, all the emphasis was on winning. Losing was not an option. So if you won, you were a winner and if you lost you were a loser. I used to think that people who made the statement "It's not whether you win or lose but how you play the game" were wimps, losers or both.

Winning, we are taught, is the American way. That philosophy has created a bunch of ill-mannered brats as witnessed by some of the American tennis players in the sports arena. Rudyard Kipling said that when you meet with triumph and disaster you "should treat those two impostors just the same." I watched Boris Becker at Wimbledon get behind Stephan Edberg two sets to love and then storm back and capture the next two sets and actually take a three to one lead with a service break in the fifth set. All he had to do to win Wimbledon for the third time was serve out. Edberg, in order to win, had to twice break the best serve in the history of Wimbledon and then hold his own serve. He succeeded!

A lesser man would have walked off the court in defeat with his head hung low, sunk into a chair and put a towel over his face. But Boris Becker climbed over the net, walked over to Edberg and embraced him. More people will remember Boris Becker and the character he showed in losing that day than if he had won and simply raised the trophy over his head in victory. His was a triumph of character over defeat.

So the game of life is not about winning and losing, it is about character, and it really *is* about how you play the game. I suggest that if you practice and put into action the concepts that are outlined in this book, you will play the game superbly and you will create success. If you live out your life in accordance with these concepts and values there is no way you can lose. Your character is not measured by winning or losing, but how you carry yourself in life.

I am not downplaying the importance of winning, but if you take these concepts as a whole then you will realize that what we are talking about is a system that will eventually lead to a successful career. Put the emphasis on the system, therefore, and the winning and losing will take care of itself.

If you place importance only on winning, then you may lose faith early in a promising career. If you place your faith in a system of concepts that build strong values and ethics, then in the long run you will be successful in every facet of life.

HOW DO I RATE? HOW CAN I IMPROVE?

WINGS_____

_____

WINNING AND LOSING_____

_____

X MARKS THE SPOT

X marks the spot. X can stand for a destination, a target, the focal point at which you direct your ambitions, dreams, efforts, and will. Never lose sight of your goals.

X can also mark the place where you stand right now. Each step we take, we take from where we are today.

Plan and dream for tomorrow, but keep your feet firmly planted in today, for that is where the power resides.

WHAT ARE MY PLANS AND DREAMS?

_____

_____

_____

Y

YOU

The art of being yourself is probably one of the most important concepts in this entire book. Not only in a career in sales but in life as well, **"To thine own self be true"** are words to live by.

We've all heard the words of the great philosophers through the ages: "The truth will set you free." "Know yourself." "The kingdom lies within." "We find our truest and best selves in our souls." Carl Jung said that there is a wonder child inside all of us. We are all born creative, spontaneous, loving, caring and compassionate beings. As we move through life the wonder child becomes wounded from life's experiences, ranging from not having needs met in early childhood on through the peer group pressures of adolescence all the way to the stressful pressures of adult responsibilities. We form layers of protection around the wonder child to keep from being further wounded.

Unfortunately, while those layers of armor can protect us from some degree of wounding, it also shuts us away from our true selves and prevents us from getting in touch with who we really are. The art of self-discovery is peeling away layers as you would peel away the skin of an onion to uncover and rediscover that wonder child.

The journey within holds mixed blessings. The initial journey is wrought with pain and frustration, but the trip is well worth the effort as you discover and express the real you. As we progress through life and move farther and farther away from that wonder child we start putting on different masks – of who we think we are, or who we think others want us to be. This sets up a vicious cycle because we feel that if others really get to know us as our true selves, they wouldn't like us. Our protective walls go up even higher and move us farther and farther away from the original wonder child within.

As you start the process of tearing the walls down by introspection you will encounter the pain of removing the illusions that you have carried around. At this point a lot of people back away and decide they would rather stay with the pain they know grows as they move farther away from the inner child and their true selves. Those who stay with the journey of self-discovery through introspection, however, reap huge rewards.

Perhaps I have gone a little deeper into the psychology of introspection and self-discovery than one might think appropriate in a sales book. However, I believe so deeply in the concept of self-discovery (I've seen the results in my own life) that I strongly suggest each one of you take that journey.

In the business world, people are naturally uncomfortable with people who are not being themselves. People are very perceptive and they instinctively know when someone is trying to be something they are not. People are very comfortable, on the other hand, with someone who is genuine, who is real. This attitude puts others at ease.

Genuineness is one of the key ingredients in establishing positive relationships in every walk of life. If it does not exist, all the rest could be an exercise in futility. I have heard it said that personal satisfaction and the level of satisfaction with other people are directly proportional.

Being yourself, and maintaining the highest level of personal integrity of which you are capable, enable you to live out the reality of Rudyard Kipling's famous poem:

IF

If you can keep your head when all about you

Are losing theirs and blaming it on you,

If you can trust yourself when all men doubt you,

But make allowance for their doubting too;

If you can wait and not be tired by waiting,

Or being lied about, don't deal in lies,

Or being hated, don't give way to hating,

And yet don't look too good, nor talk too wise:

If you can dream – and not make dreams your master;

If you can think – and not make thoughts your aim;

If you can meet with Triumph and Disaster

And treat those two impostors just the same;

If you can bear to hear the truth you've spoken

Twisted by Knaves to make a trap for fools,

Or watch the things you gave your life to, broken,

And stoop and build 'em up with worn-out tools:

If you can make one heap of all your winnings

And risk it on one turn of pitch-and-toss,

And lose, and start again at your beginnings

And never breathe a word about your loss;

If you can force your heart and nerve and sinew

To serve your turn long after they are gone,

And so hold on when there is nothing in you

Except the Will which says to them: 'Hold on!'

If you can talk with crowds and keep your virtue,

Or walk with Kings – nor lose the common touch,

If neither foes nor loving friends can hurt you,

If all men count with you, but none too much;

If you can fill the unforgiving minute

With sixty seconds' worth of distance run,

Yours is the Earth and everything that's in it,

And – which is more – you'll be a Man, my son!

There is no more satisfying experience than to be

truly yourself, and this satisfaction will carry forward into

your dealings with others. Let's face it, nobody wants to

do business with someone who makes them feel uncomfortable.

There is no greater tragedy than to go through life never knowing who you are, and no greater joy than living as your best self.

Don't miss the trip.

HOW DO I RATE? HOW CAN I IMPROVE?

YOU_____

_____

_____

_____

Z

ZERO

Zero represents the sum total your commissions will amount to, if you fail to follow the simple guidelines in this book!

CHECKLIST FOR SUCCESS

1. Have you established goals for your career, and, if so, how are you progressing?

2. Are you moving towards physical fitness by working out four times a week?

3. How are you handling your emotions?

4. Are you asking your customers for their business?

5. Are you studying to keep abreast of your industry?

6. Are you treating everyone with courtesy and respect regardless of their position?

7. Are you covering all decision makers?

8. Are you maintaining your values and ethics in all your dealings?

9. Are you taking care of your personal grooming, your clothes, and your car?

10. Are you being creative by offering new ideas?

11. Are you listening more and talking less?

12. Are you moving closer to the real you?

Zero

ZERO- Could be your sales commission if you don't build positive relationships based on the values found in this book.

AFTERWORD

THE ROAD NOT TAKEN

Two roads diverged in a yellow wood,
And sorry I could not travel both
And be one traveler, long I stood
And looked down one as far as I could
To where it bent in the undergrowth;
Then took the other, as just as fair,
And having perhaps the better claim,
Because it was grassy and wanted wear;
Though as for that the passing there
Had worn them really about the same,
And both that morning equally lay
In leaves no step had trodden black.
Oh, I kept the first for another day!
Yet knowing how way leads on to way,
I doubted if I should ever come back.
I shall be telling this with a sigh
Somewhere ages and ages hence:
Two roads diverged in a wood, and I-
I took the one less traveled by,
And that has made all the difference.

Robert Frost